# ADULT COLORING BOOK
*Over Sixty Beautiful Images.*

Let the relaxation begin here!

Our ultimate aim at Sweet Serenity Publishing is to bring you a little serenity - should you need it.

We design our products with your satisfaction in mind, and hope you enjoy this adult colouring book.

As well as the fifty main images that make up this book, we have included a bonus section of eleven images which were hand drawn on paper and turned into digital images.

We hope they bring you some pleasure.

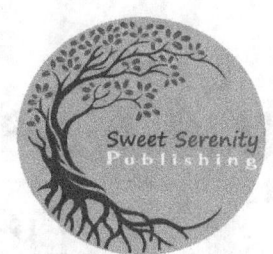

Copyright © 2020 Sweet Serenity Publishing

Contact -- sweetserenitypublishing@gmail.com

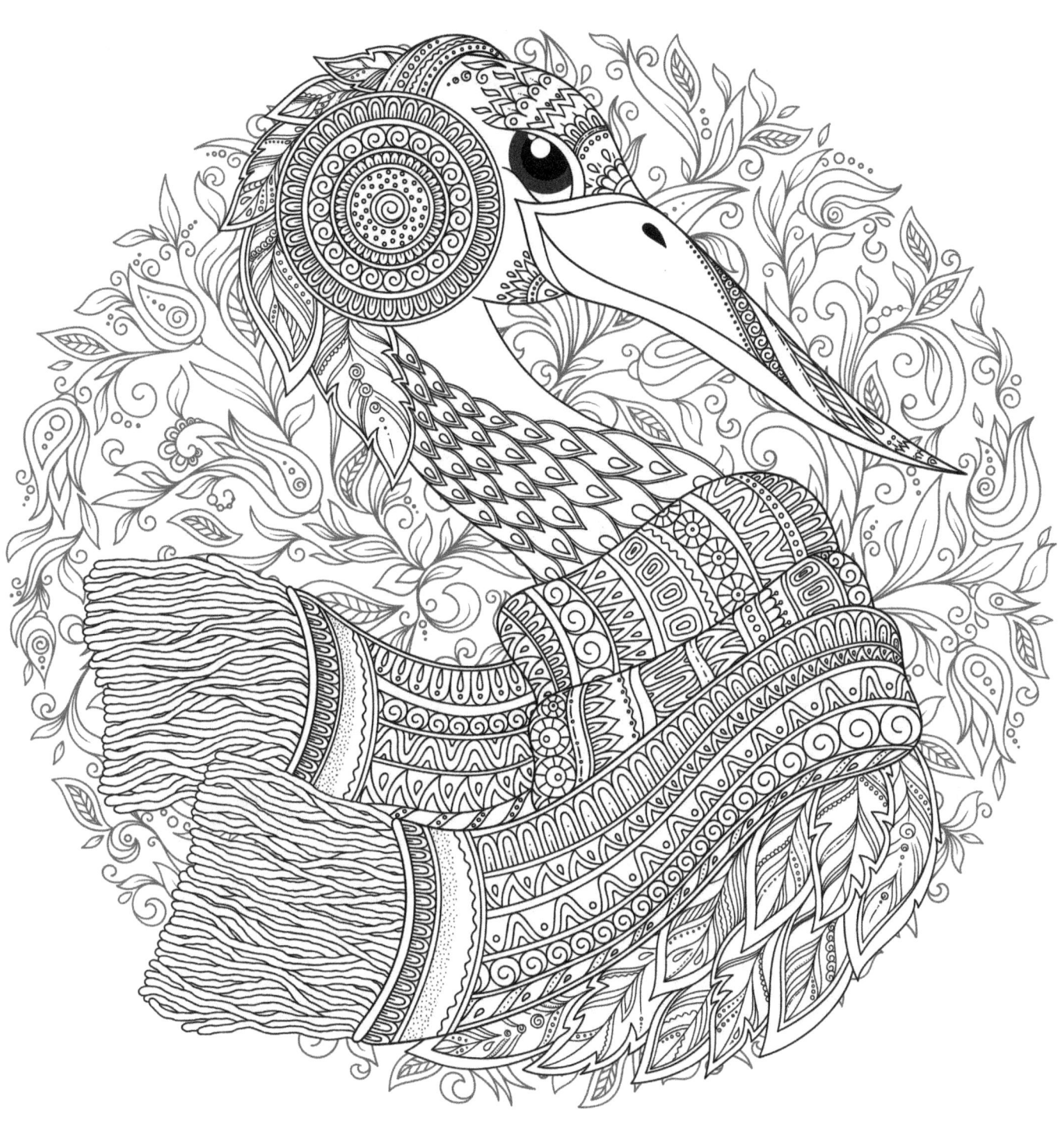

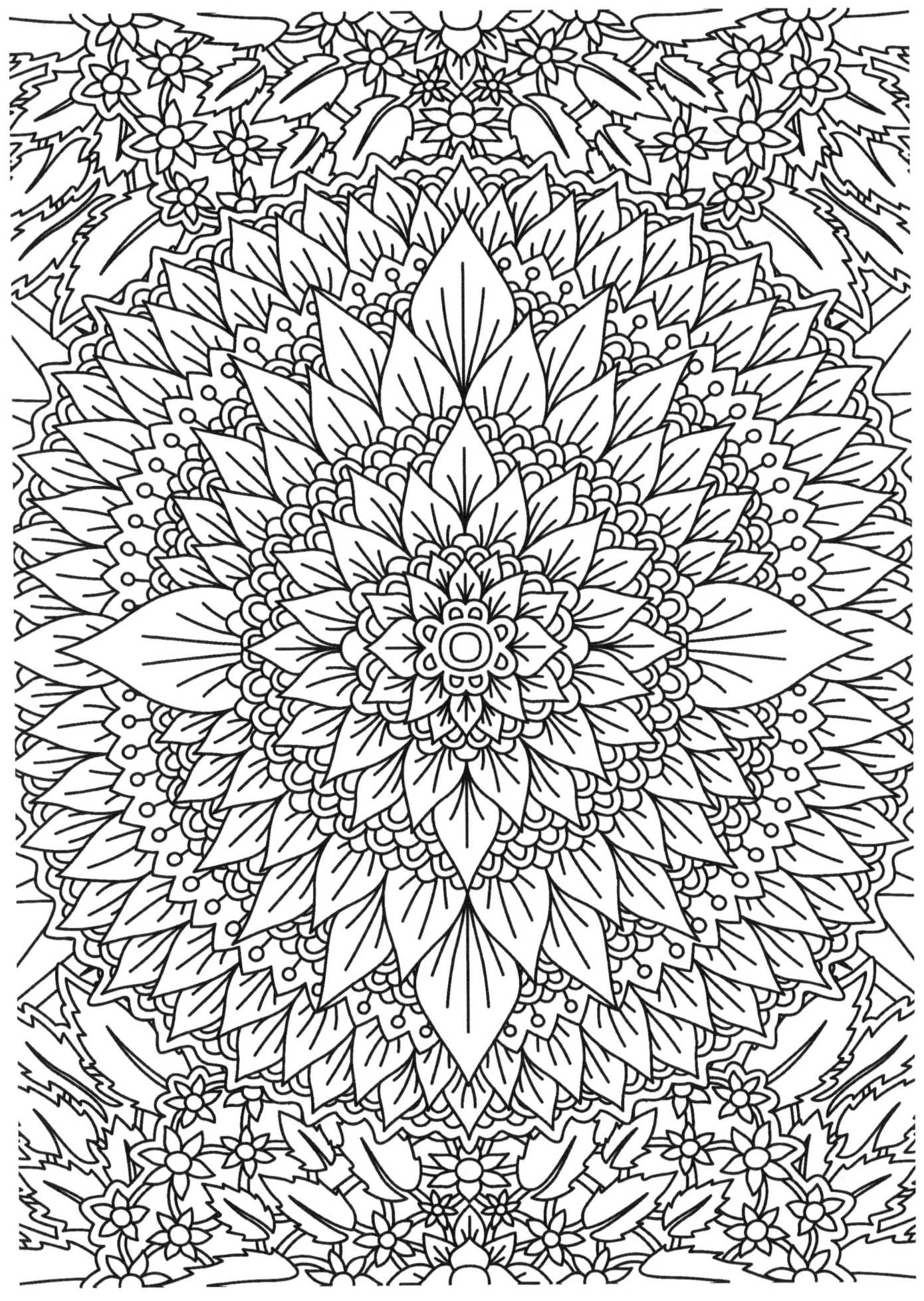

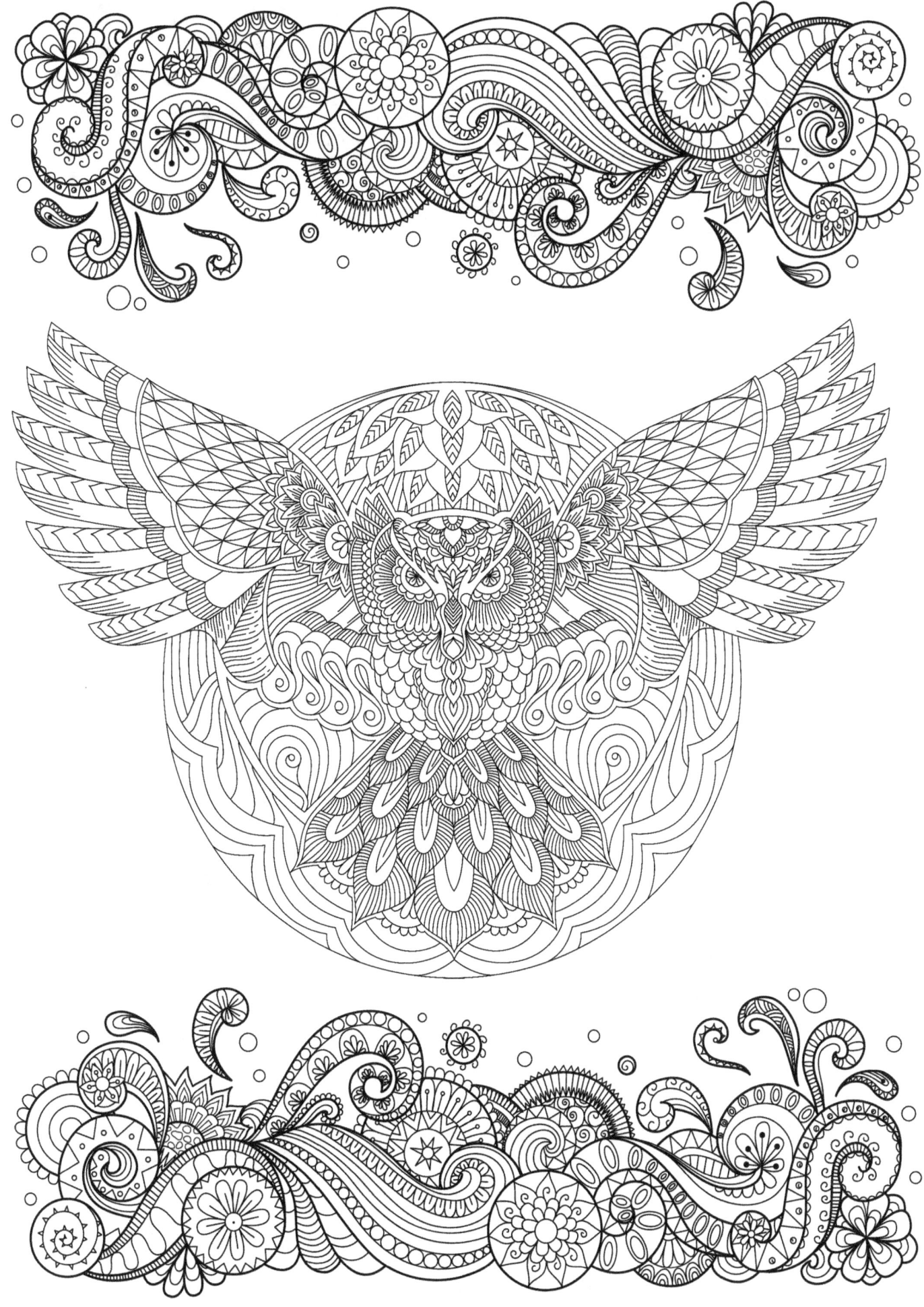

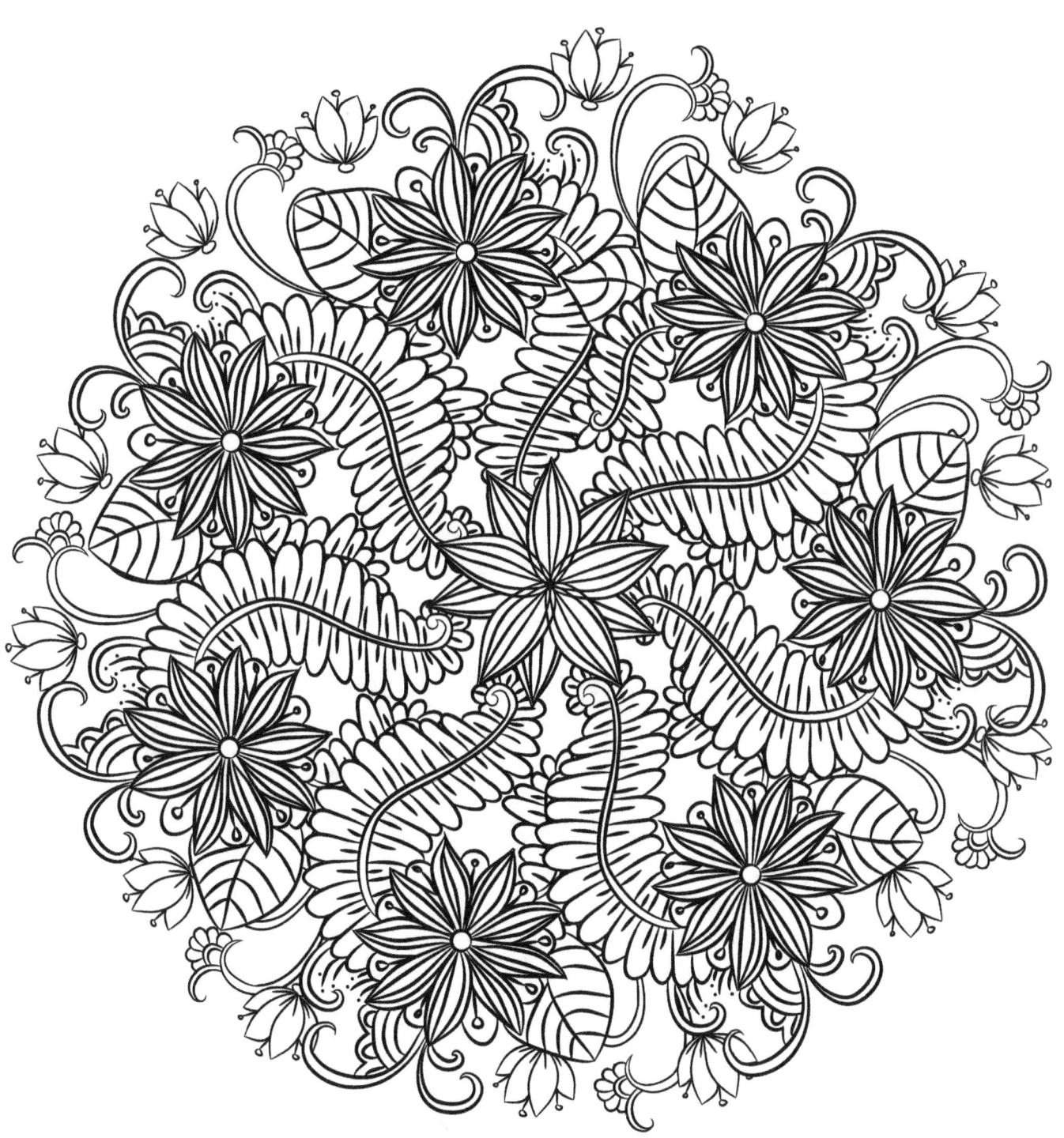

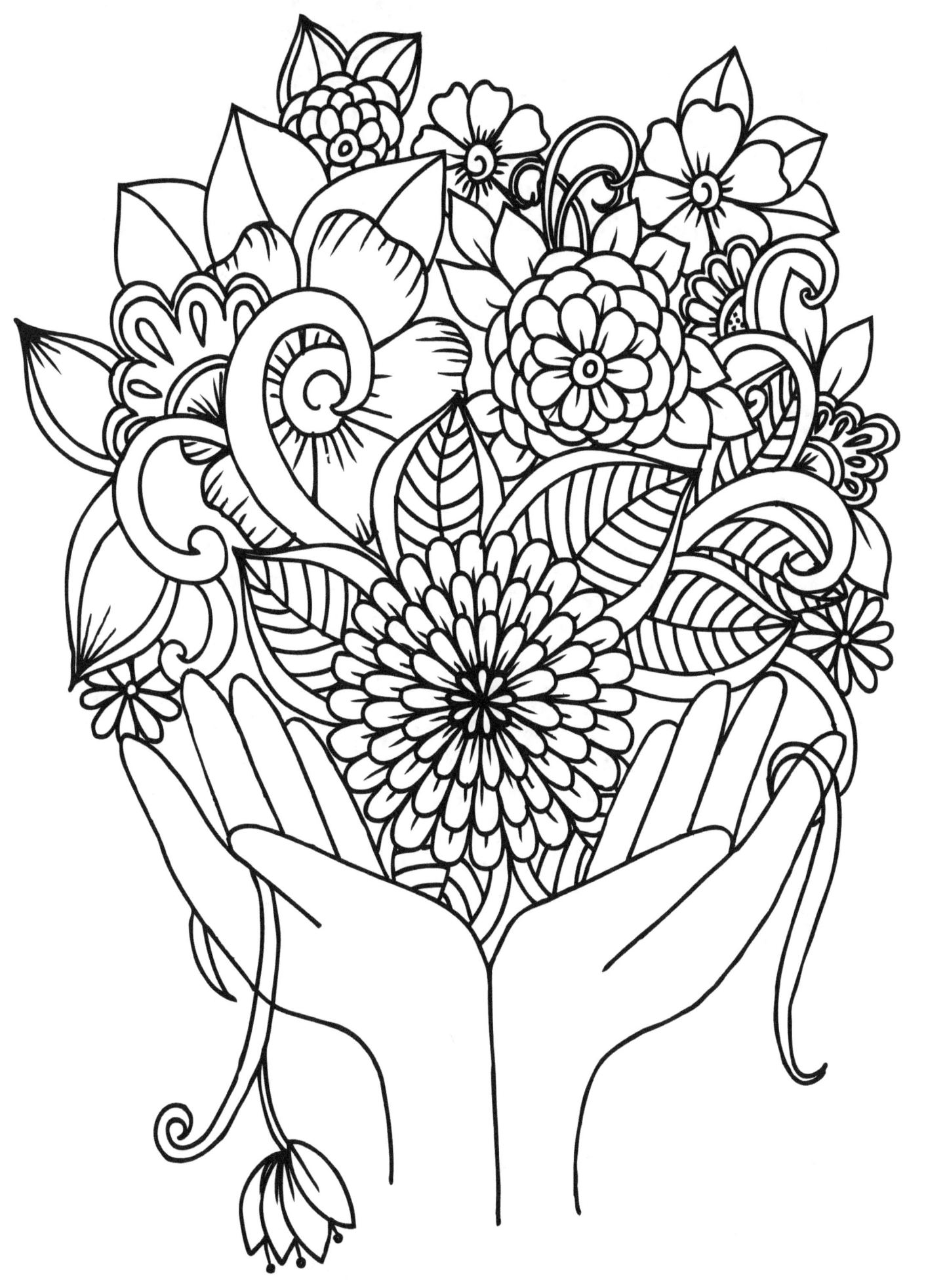

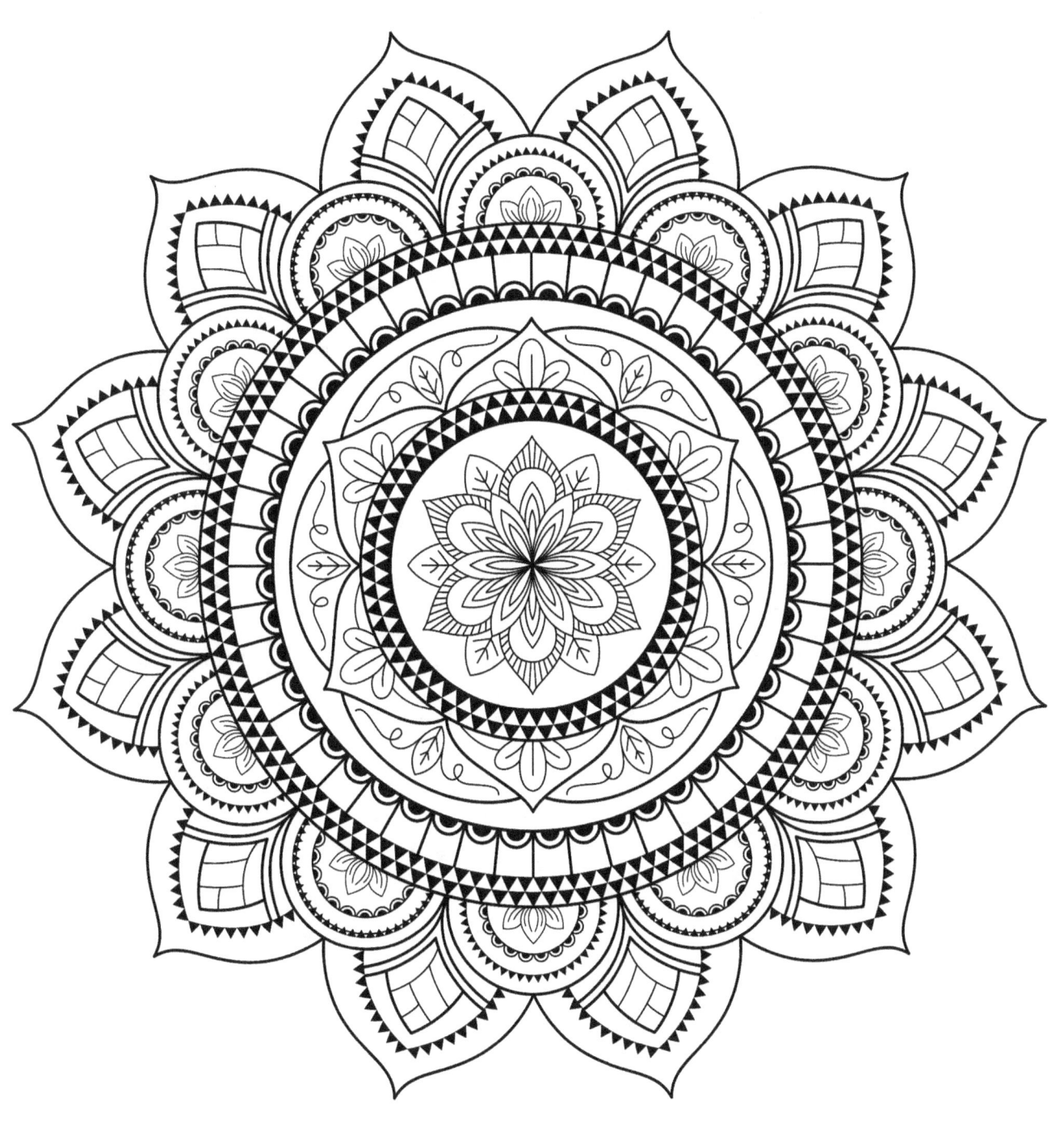

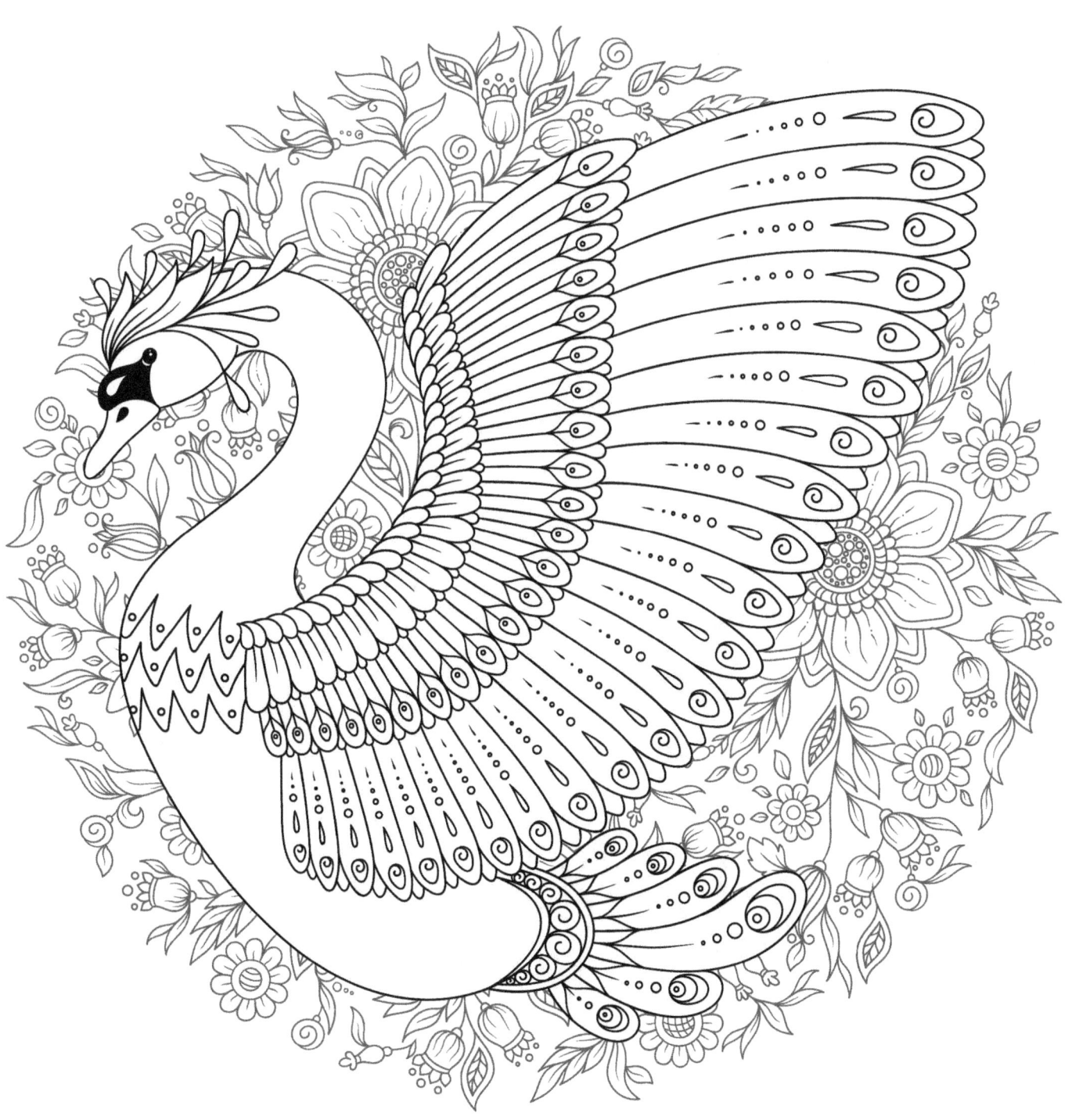

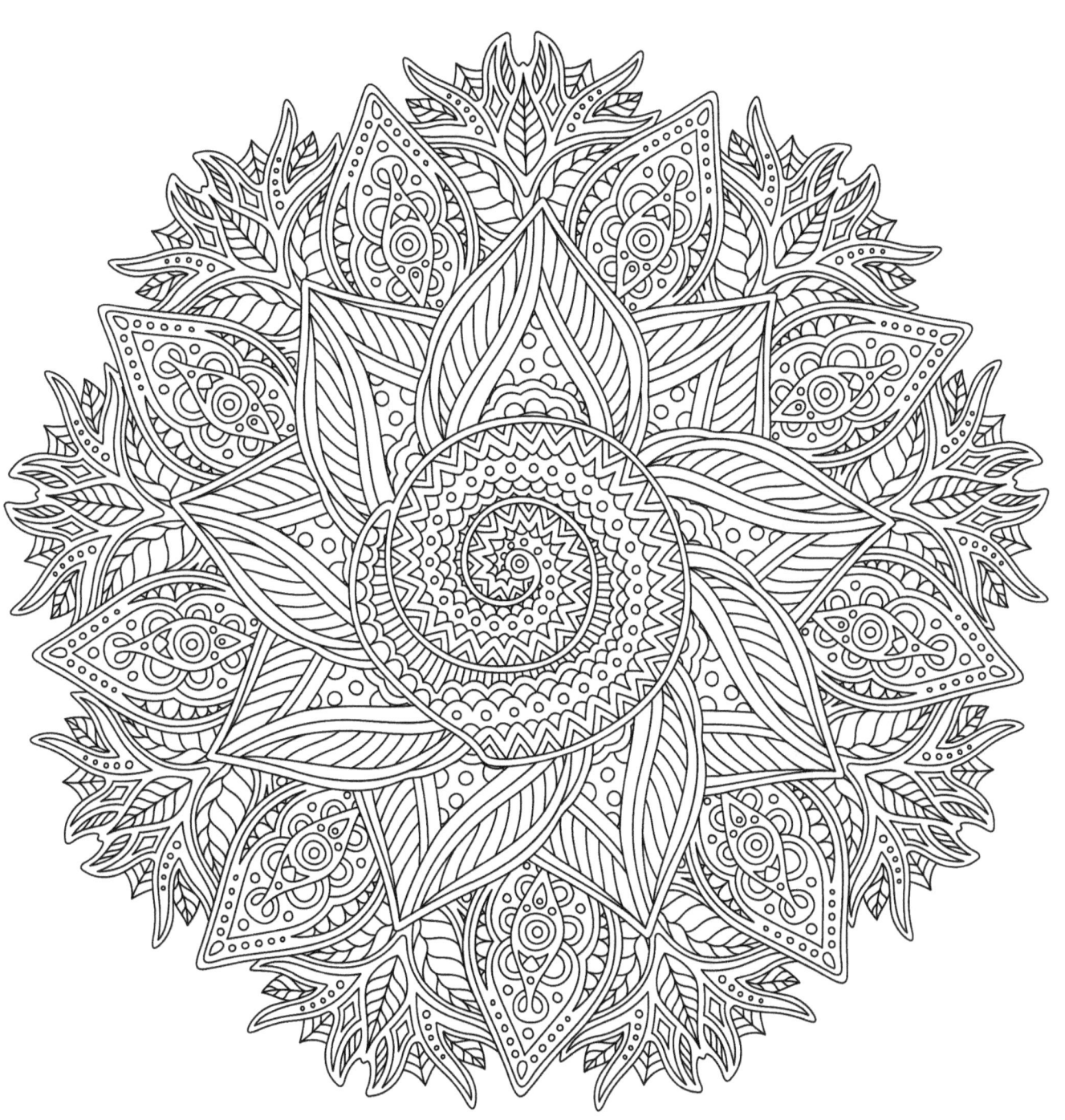

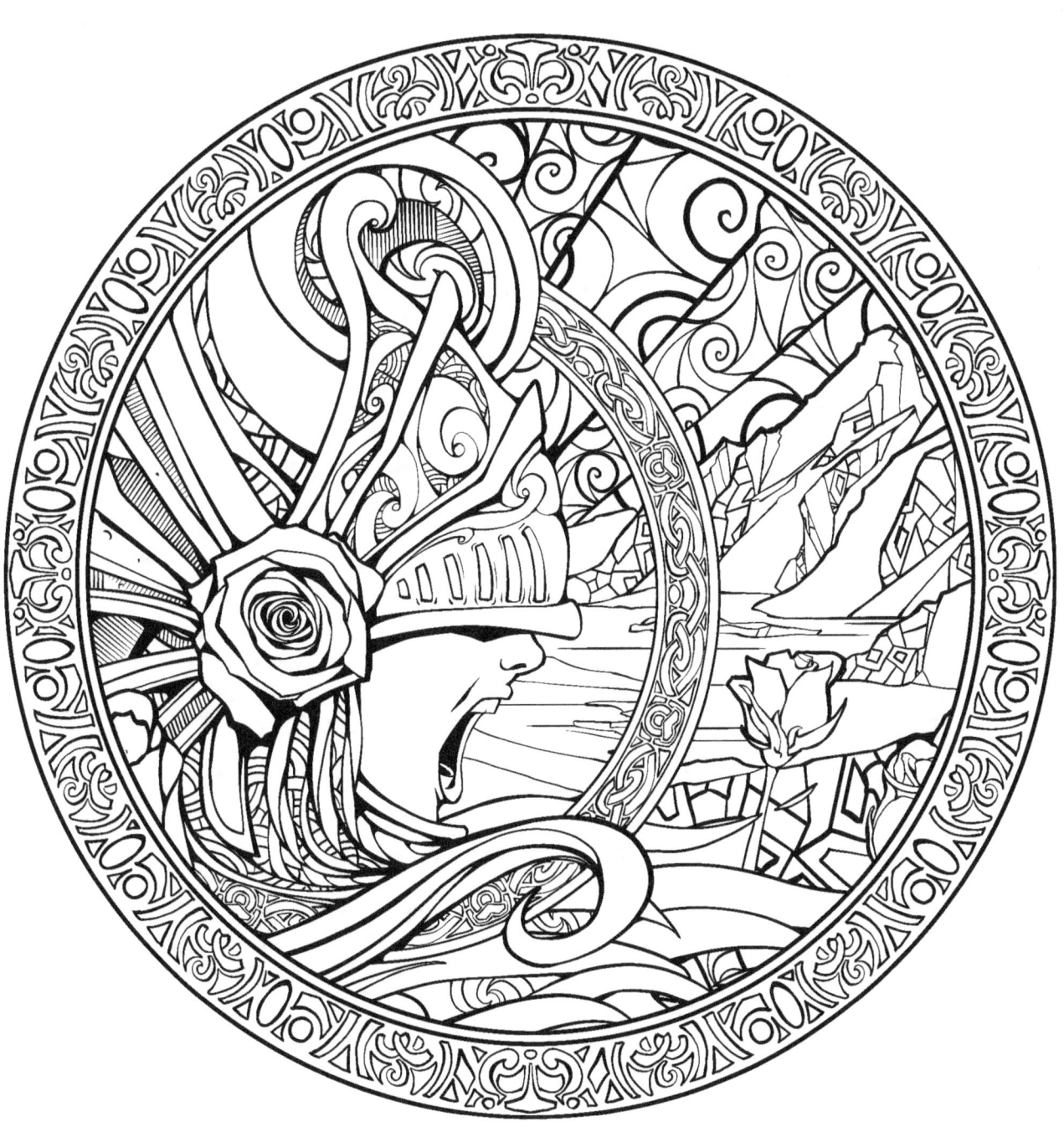

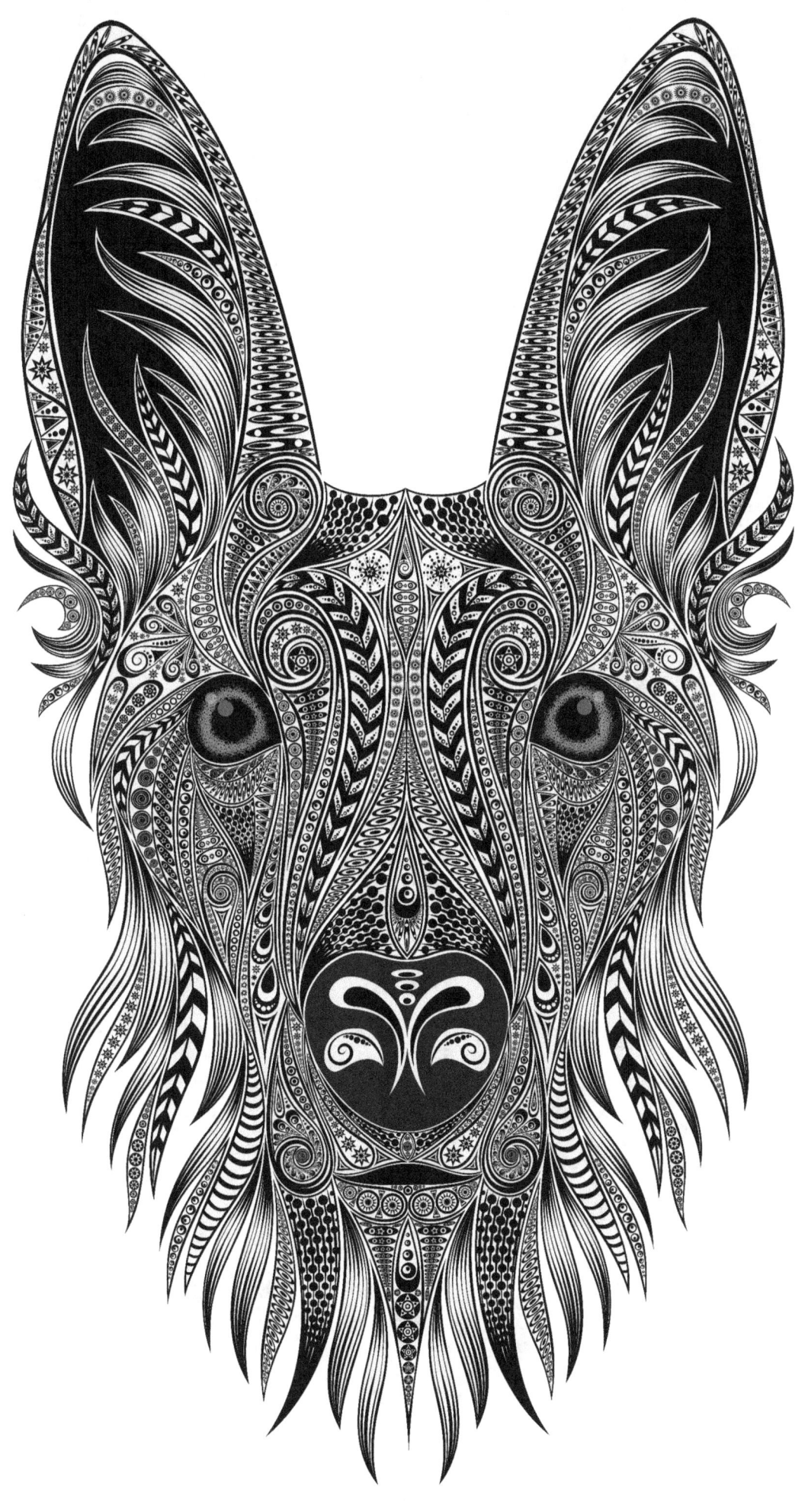

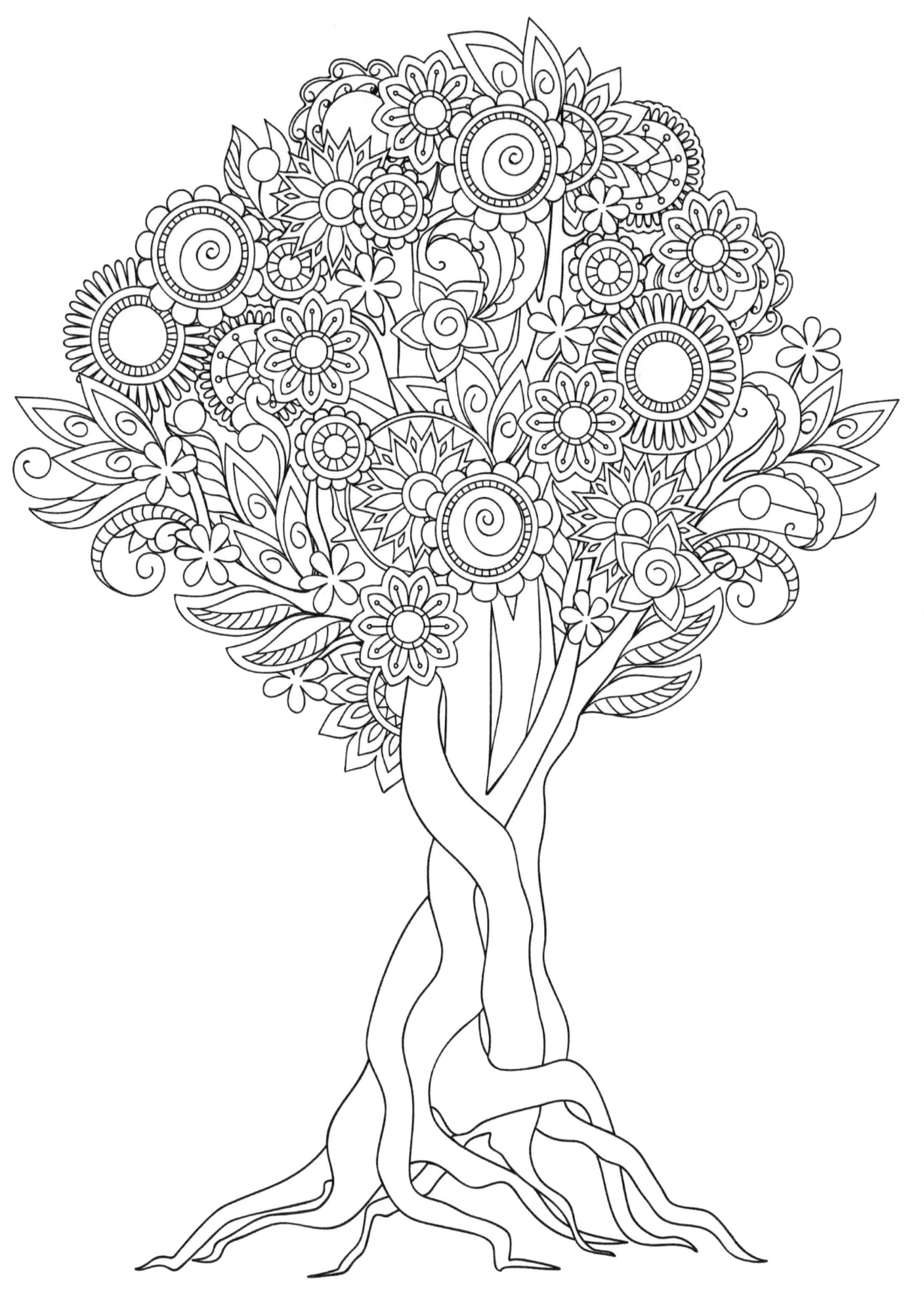

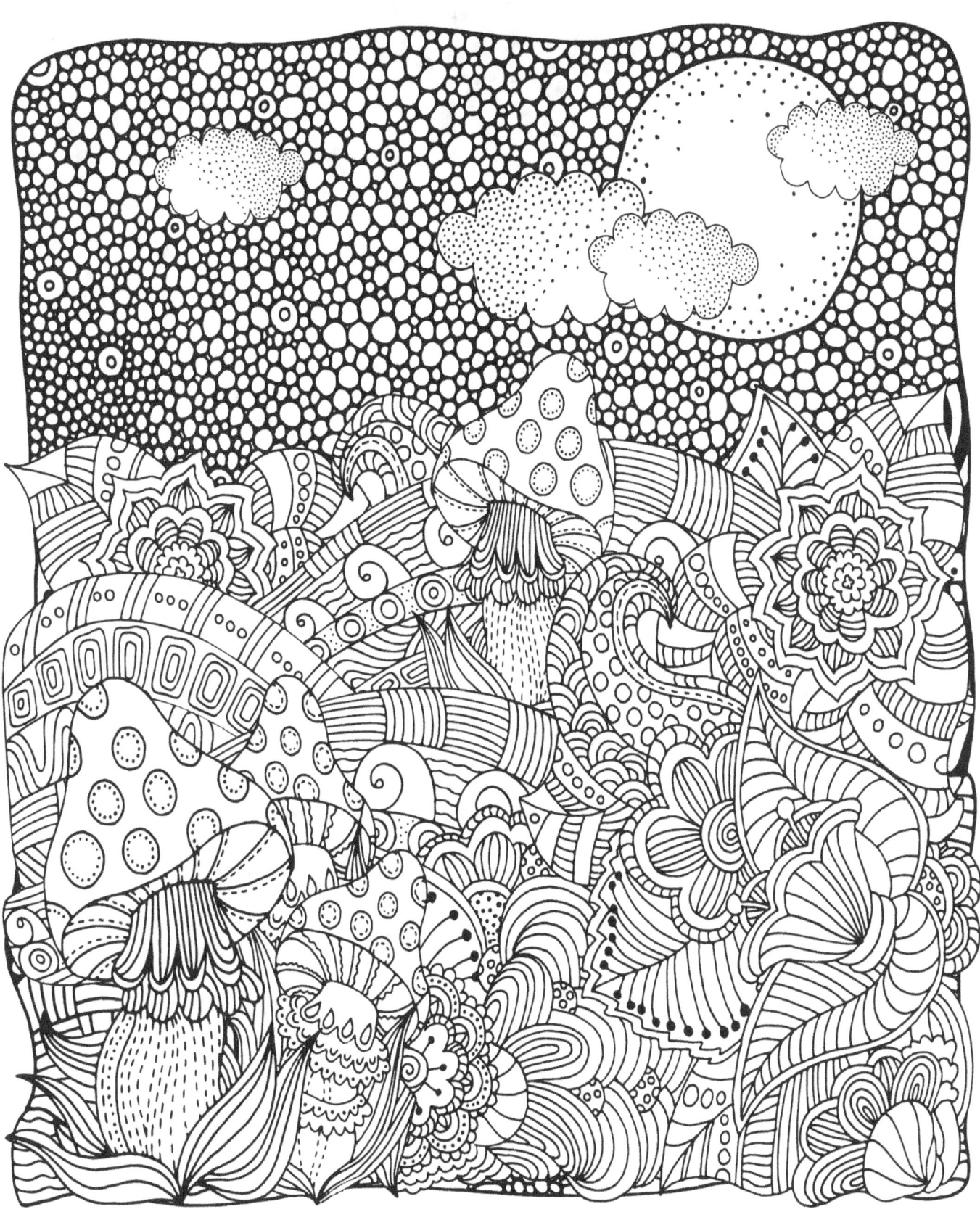

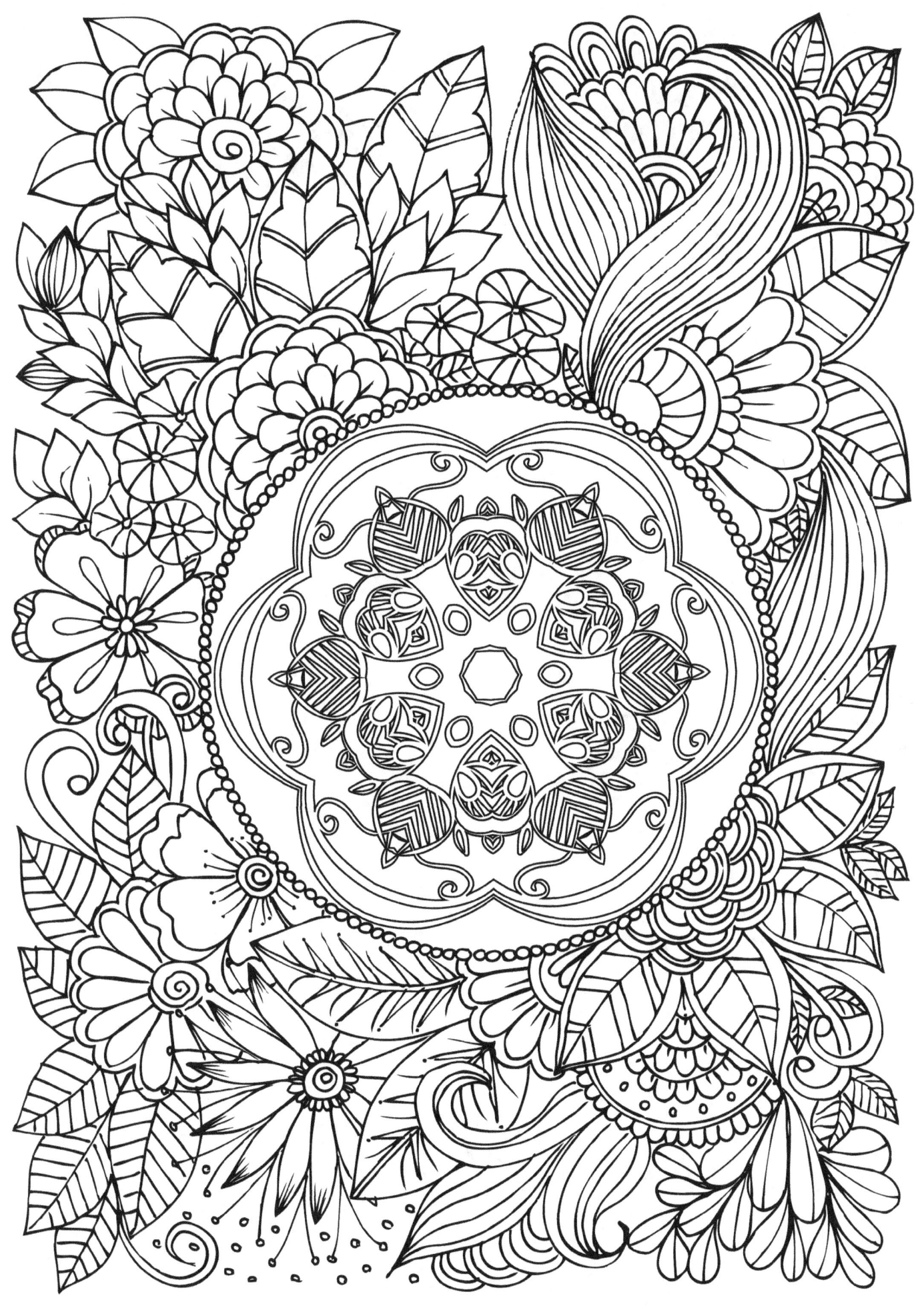

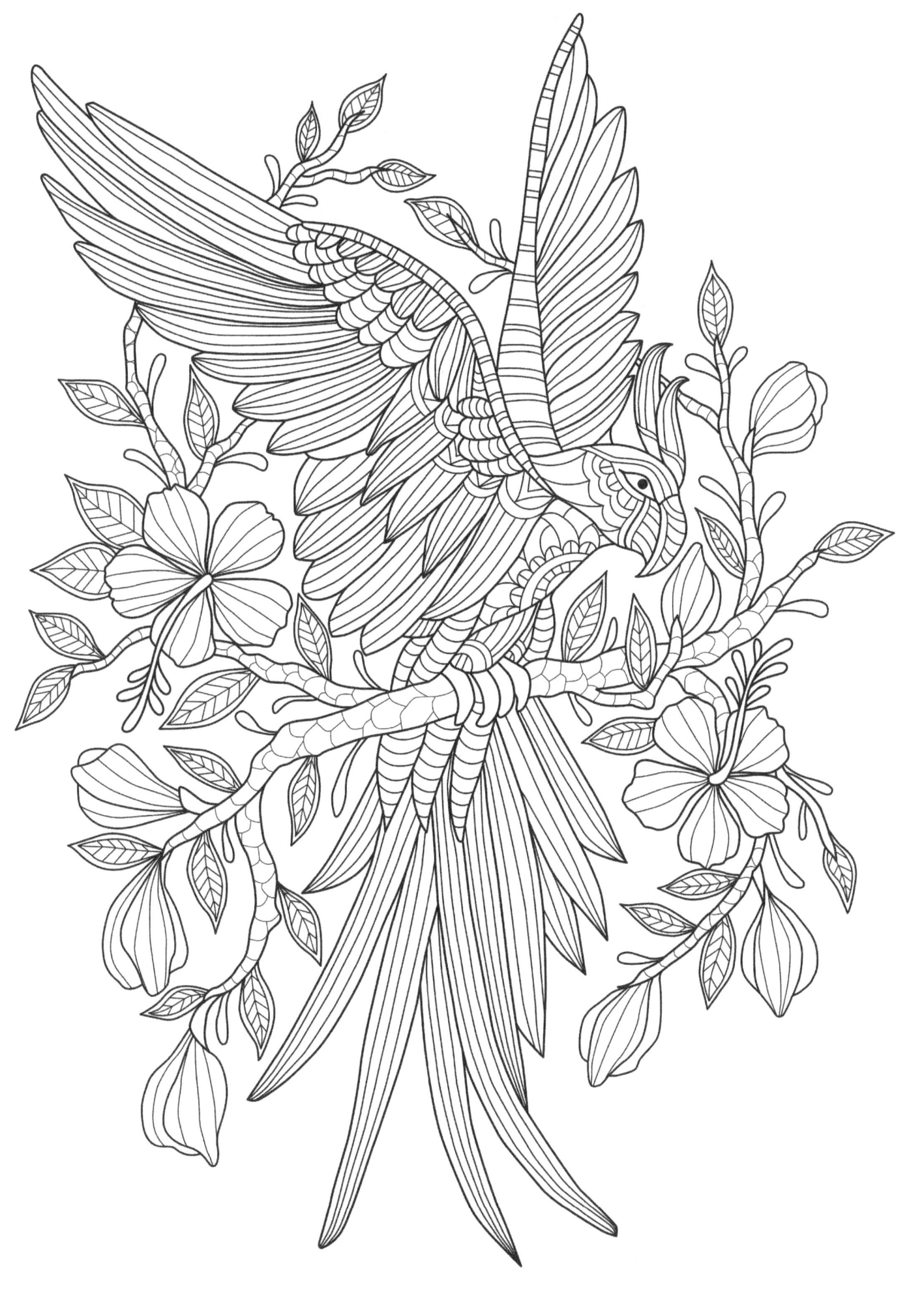

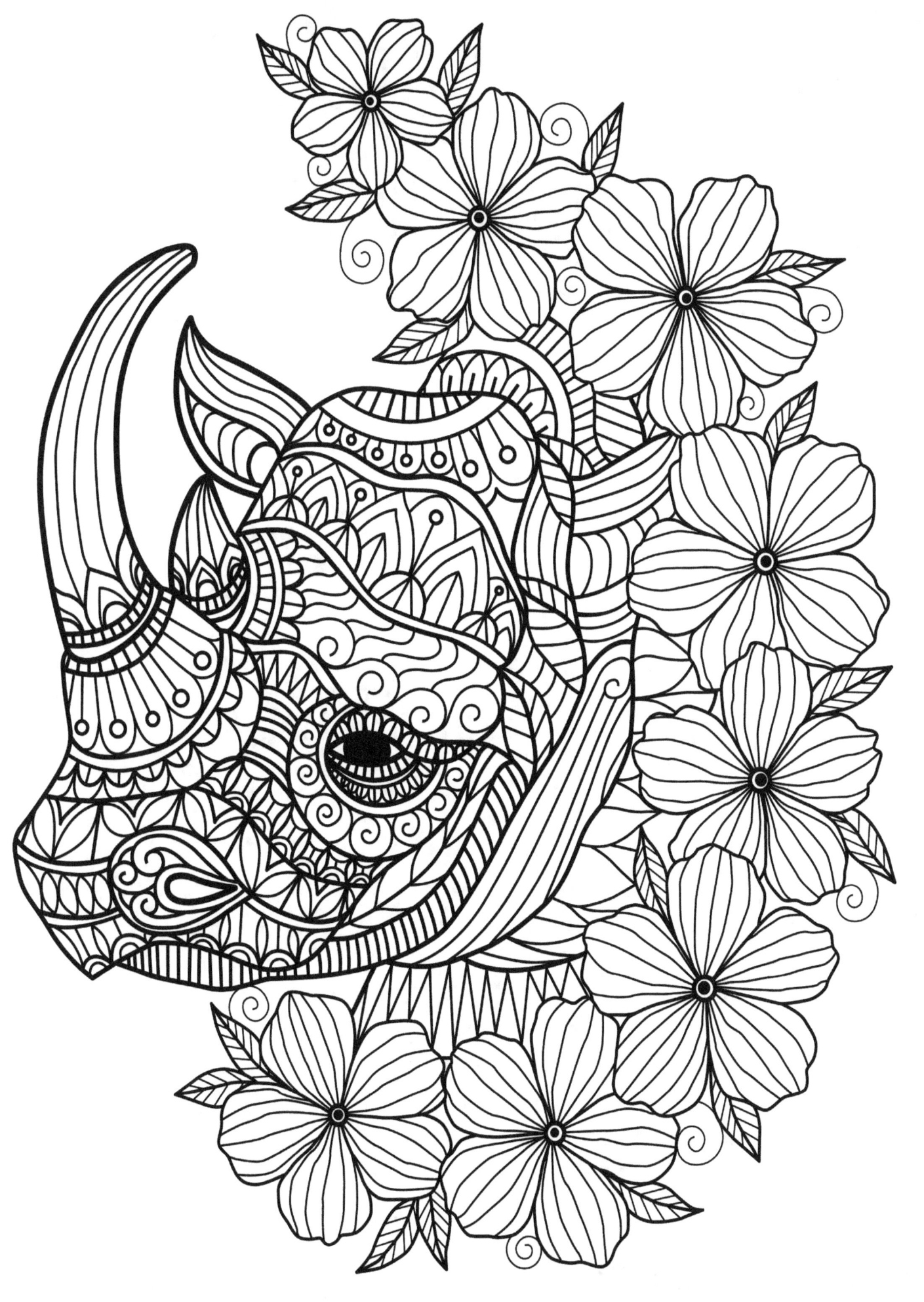

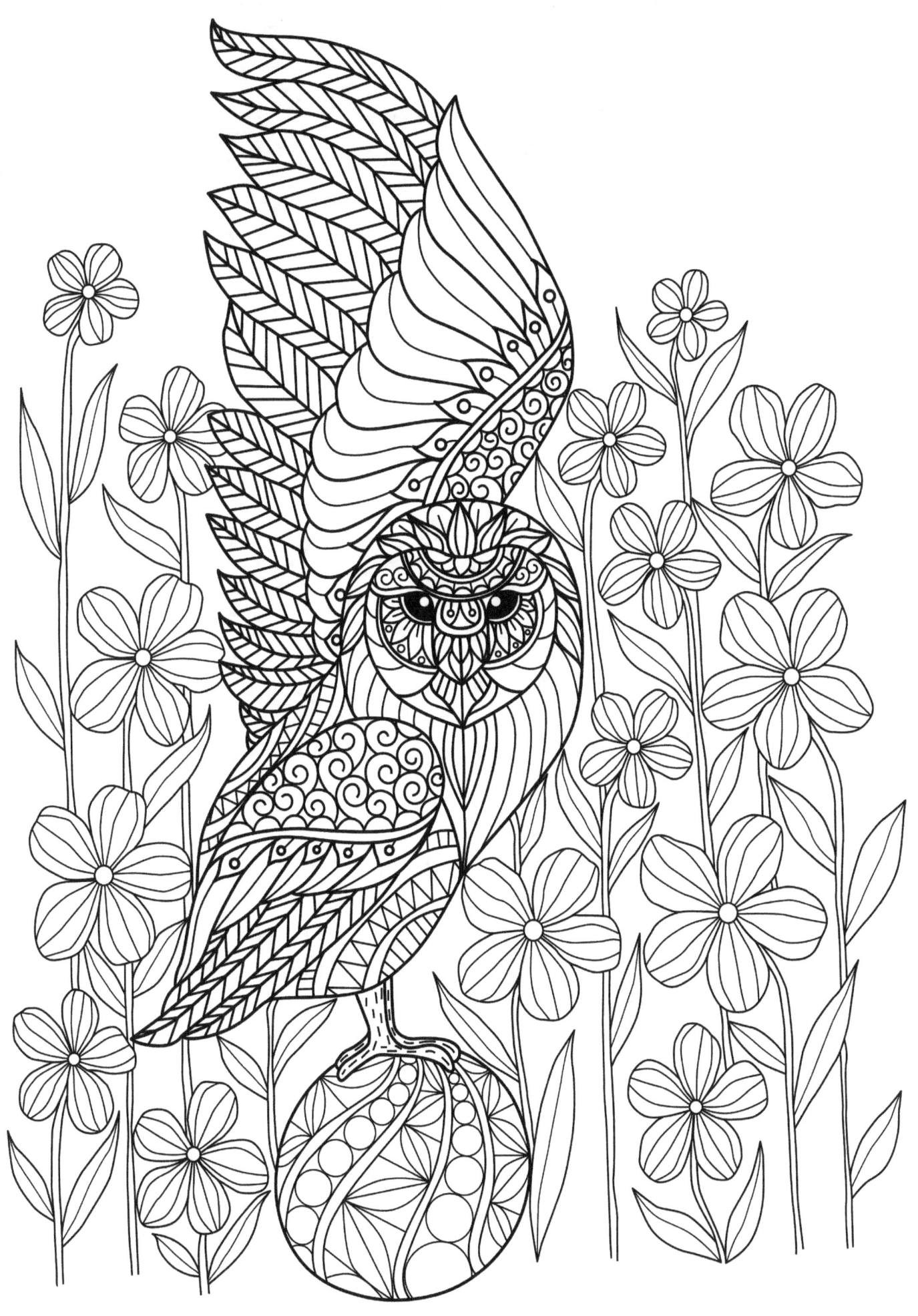

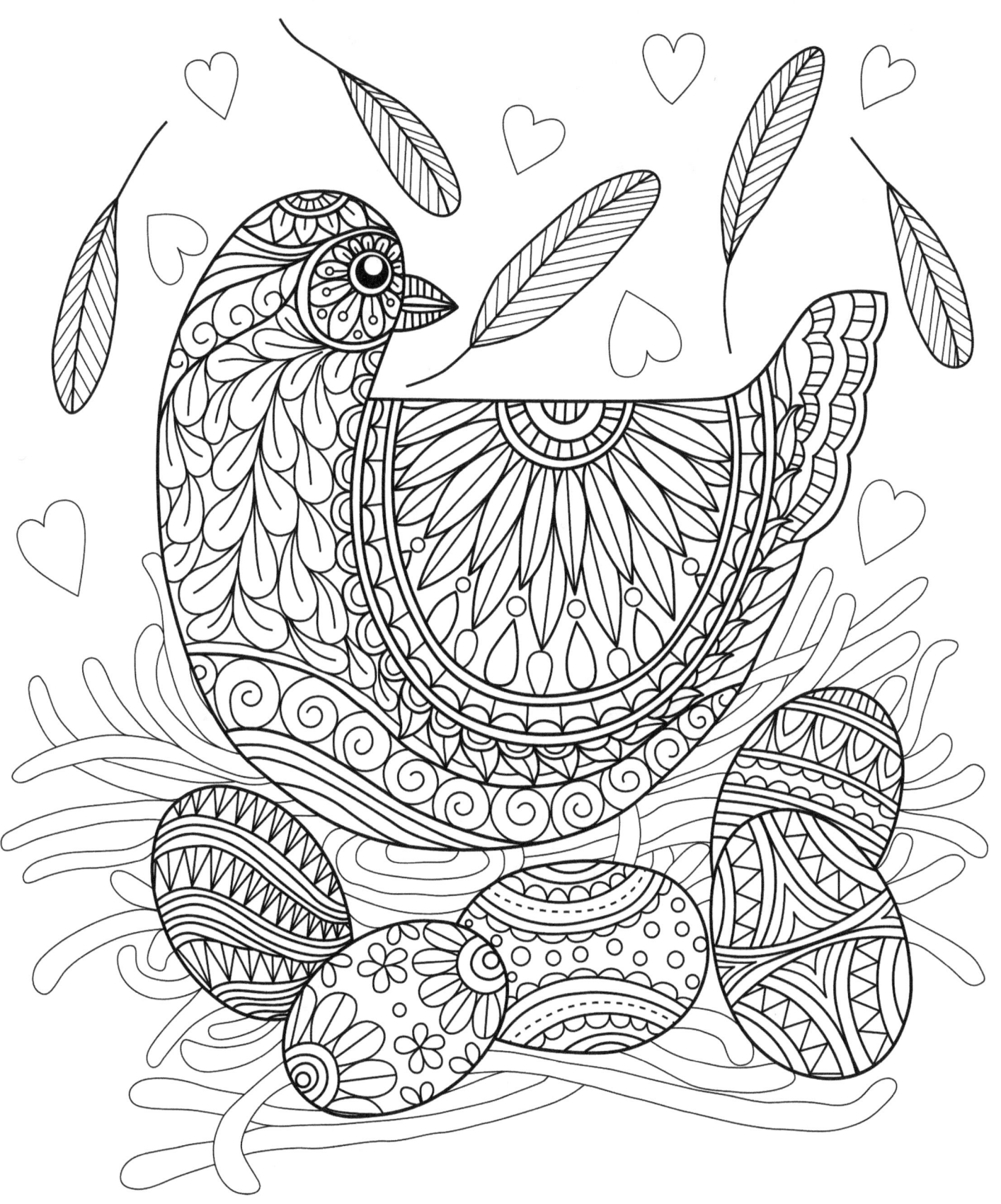

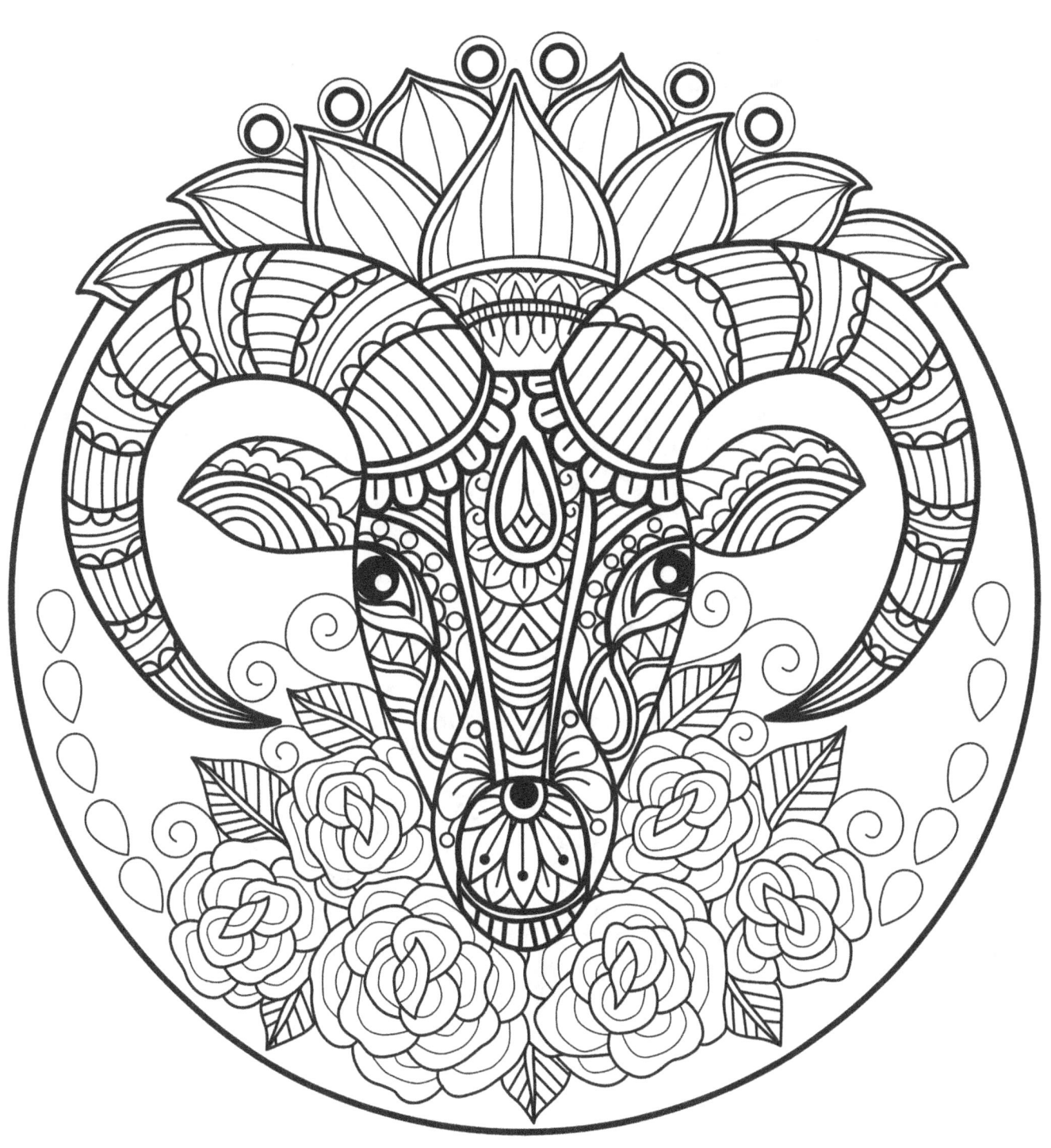

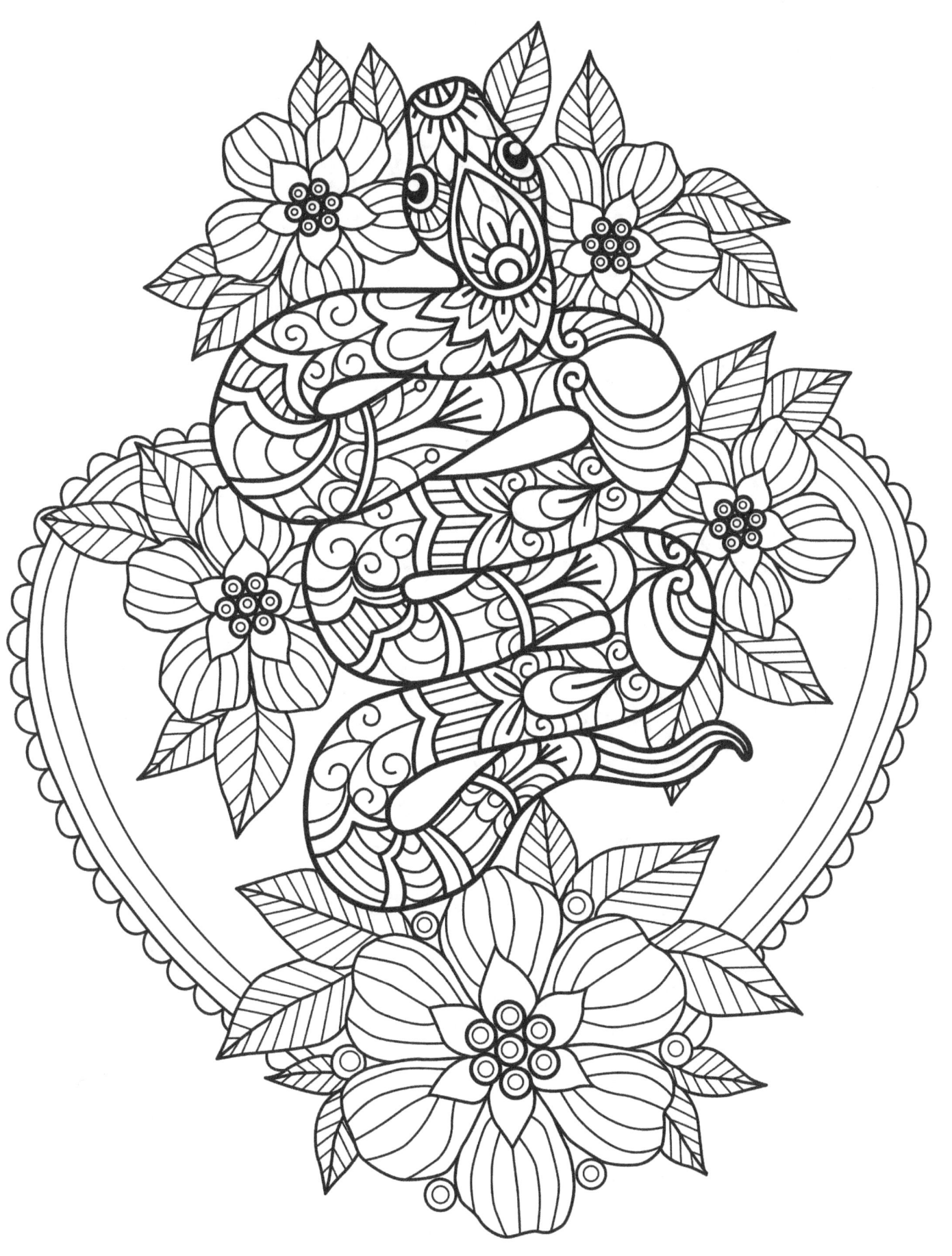

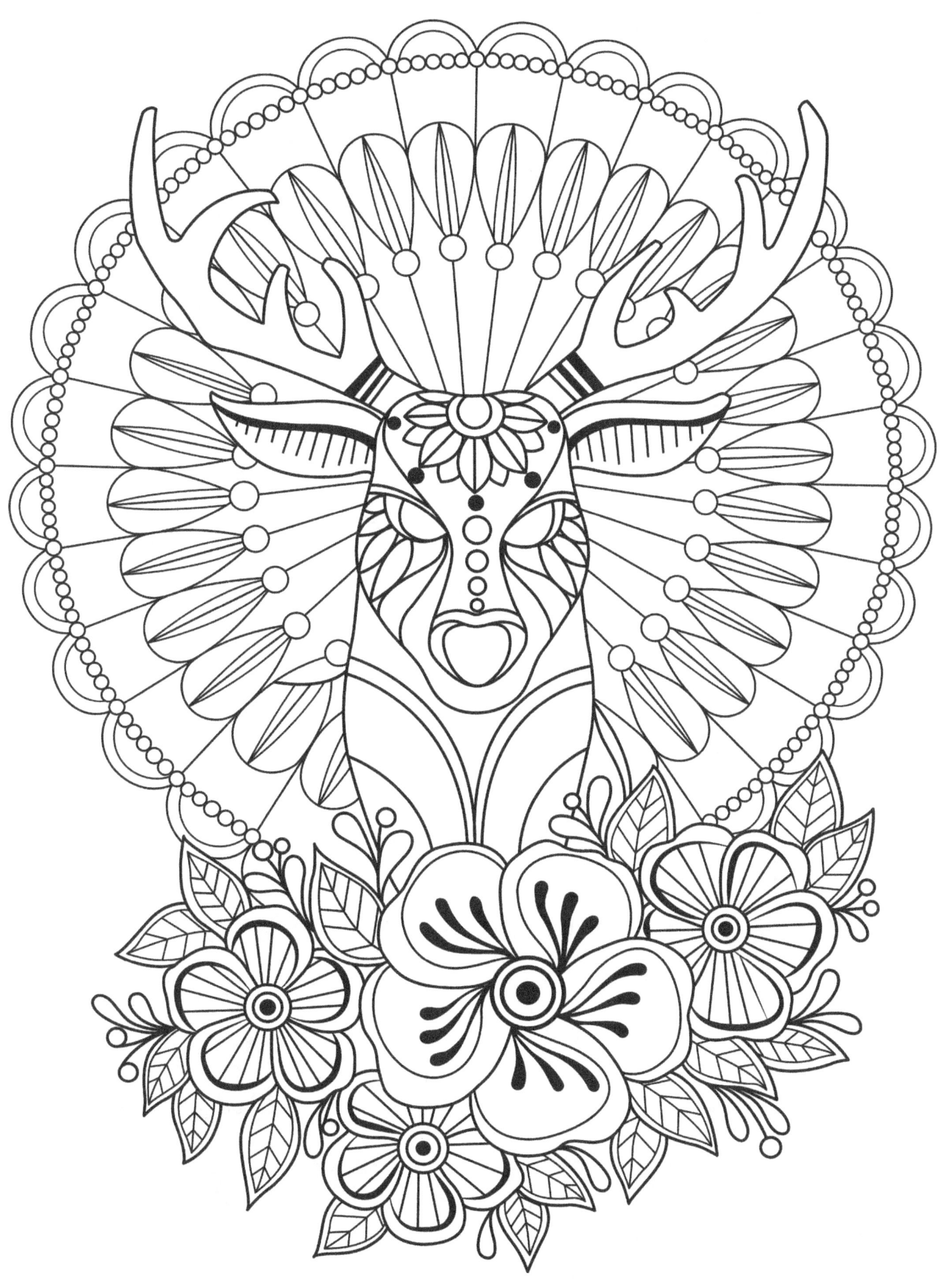

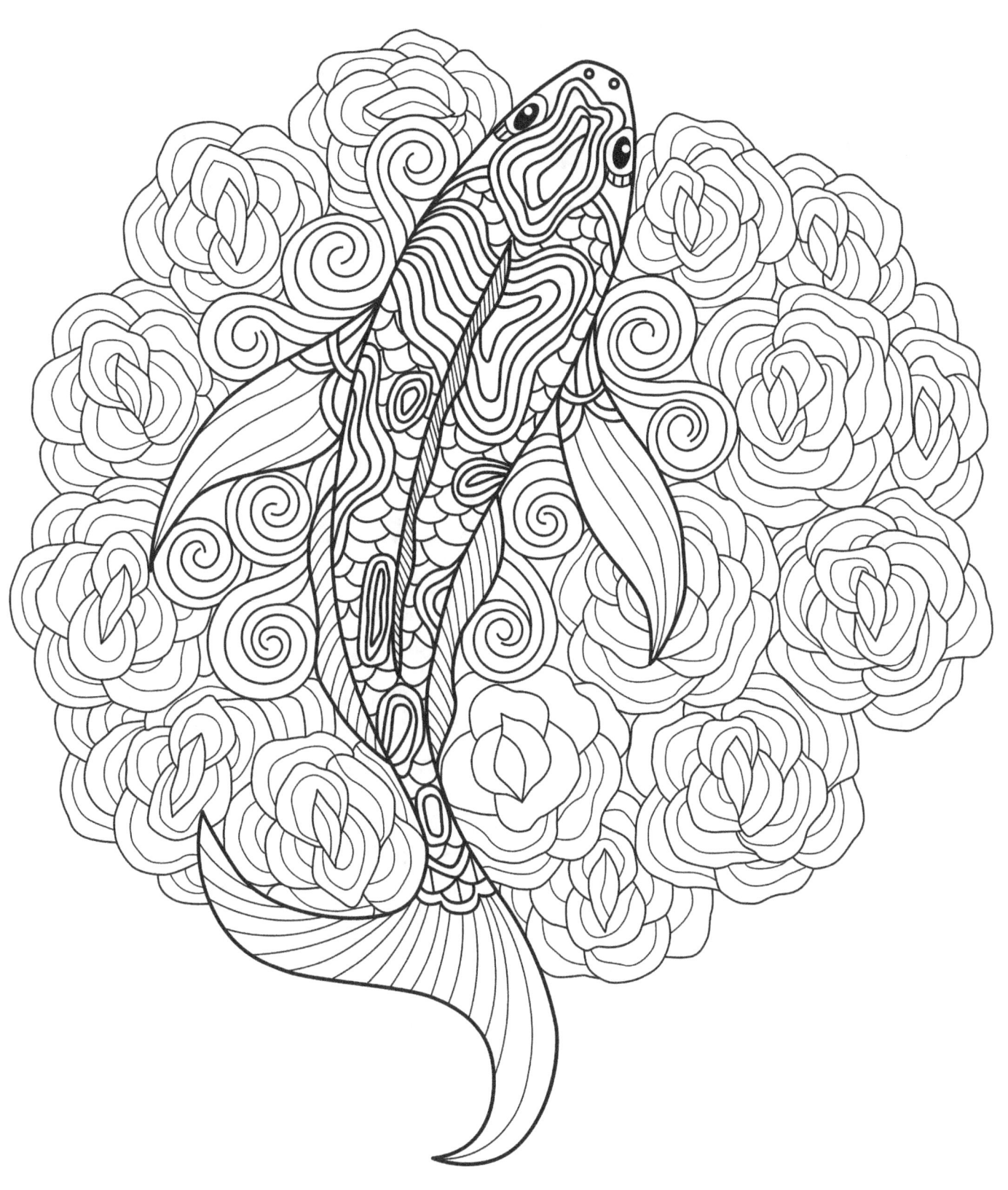

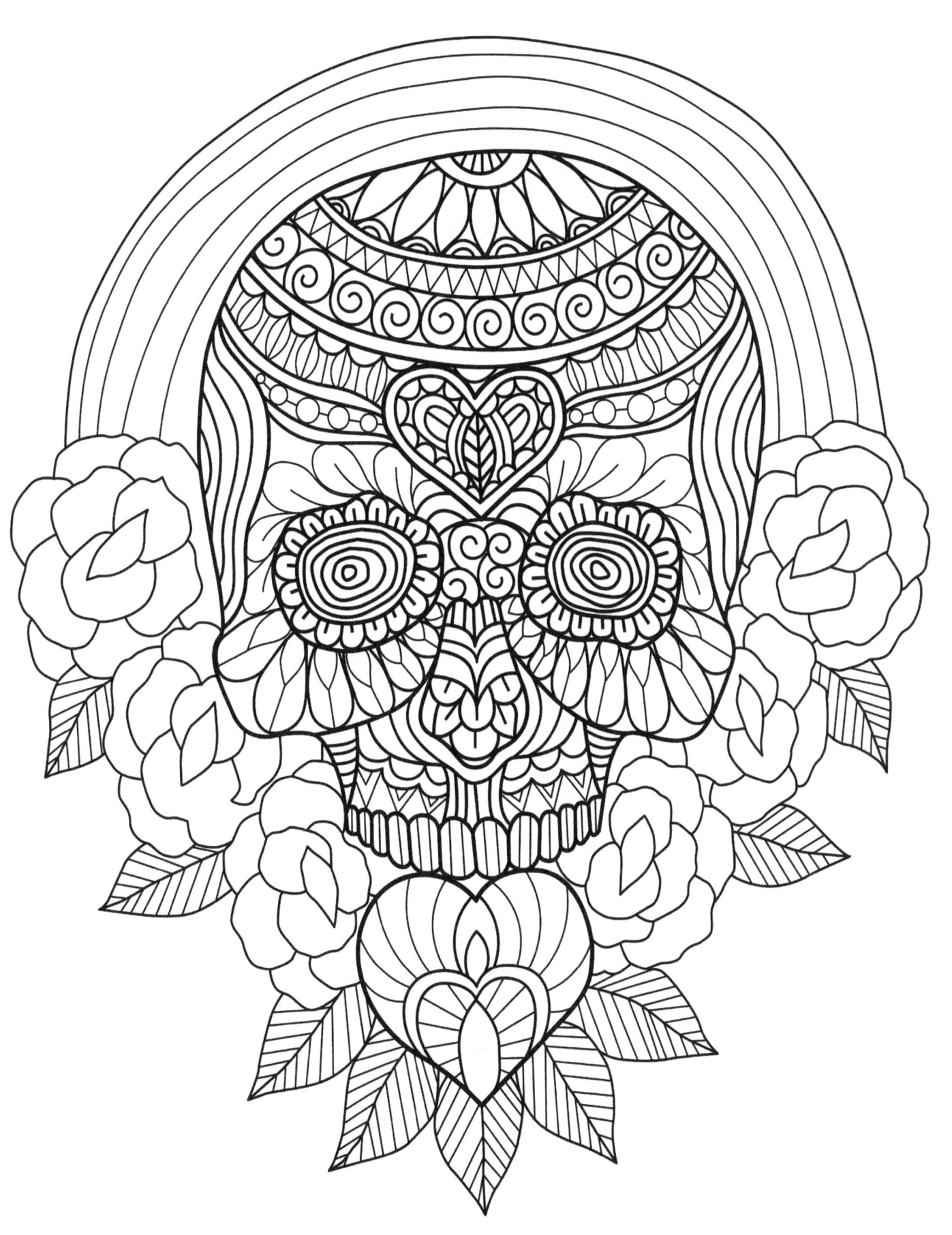

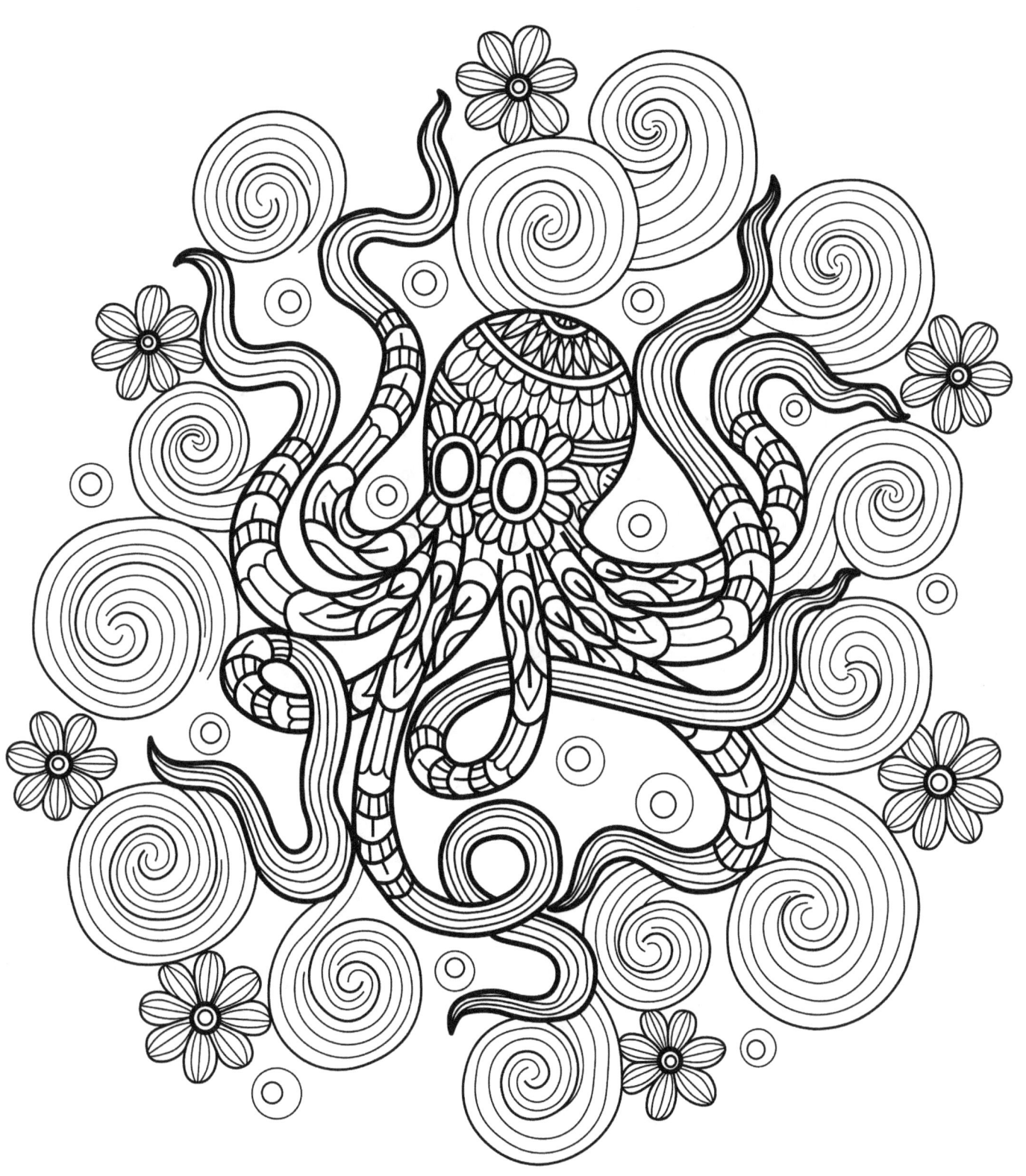

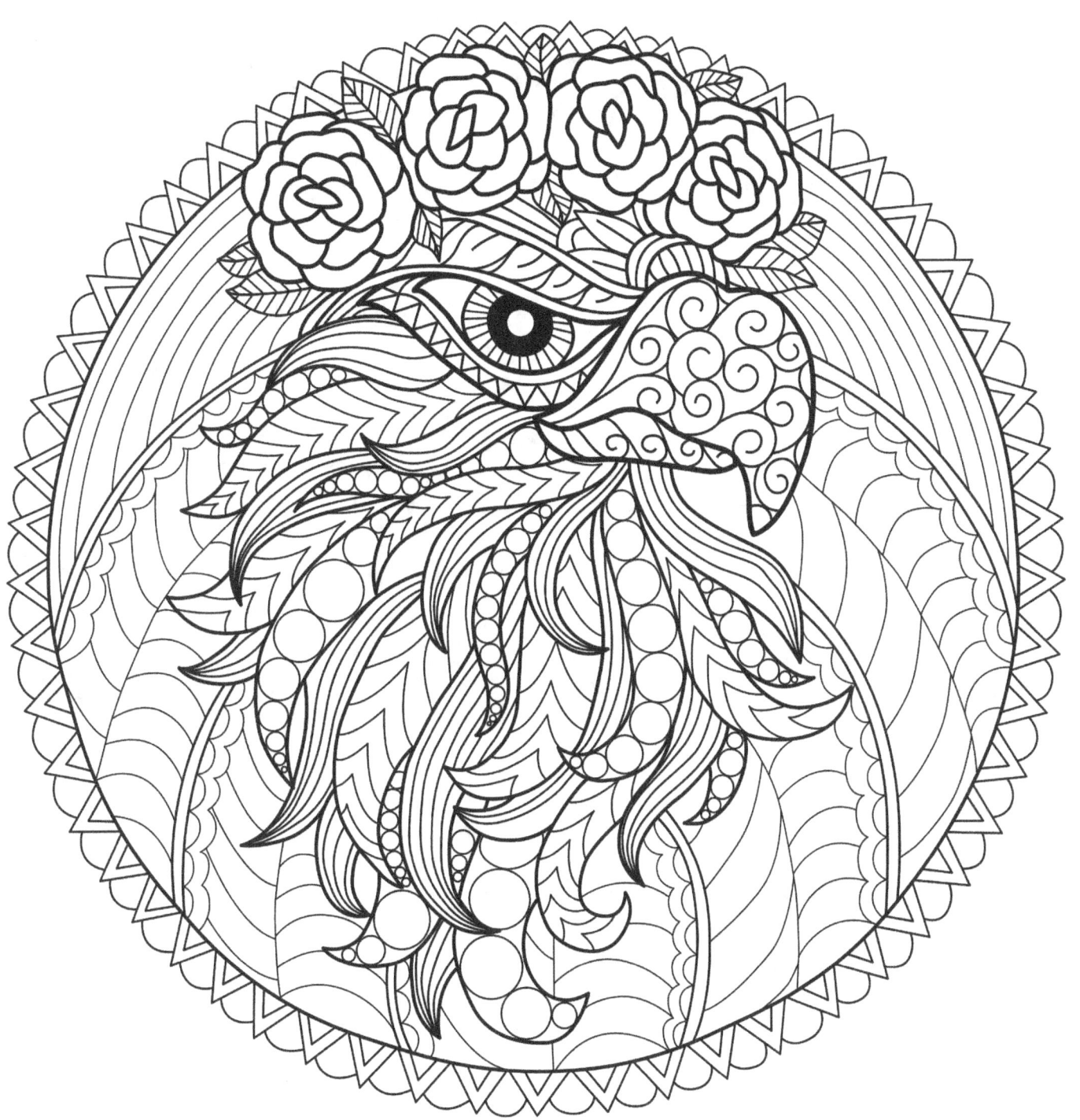

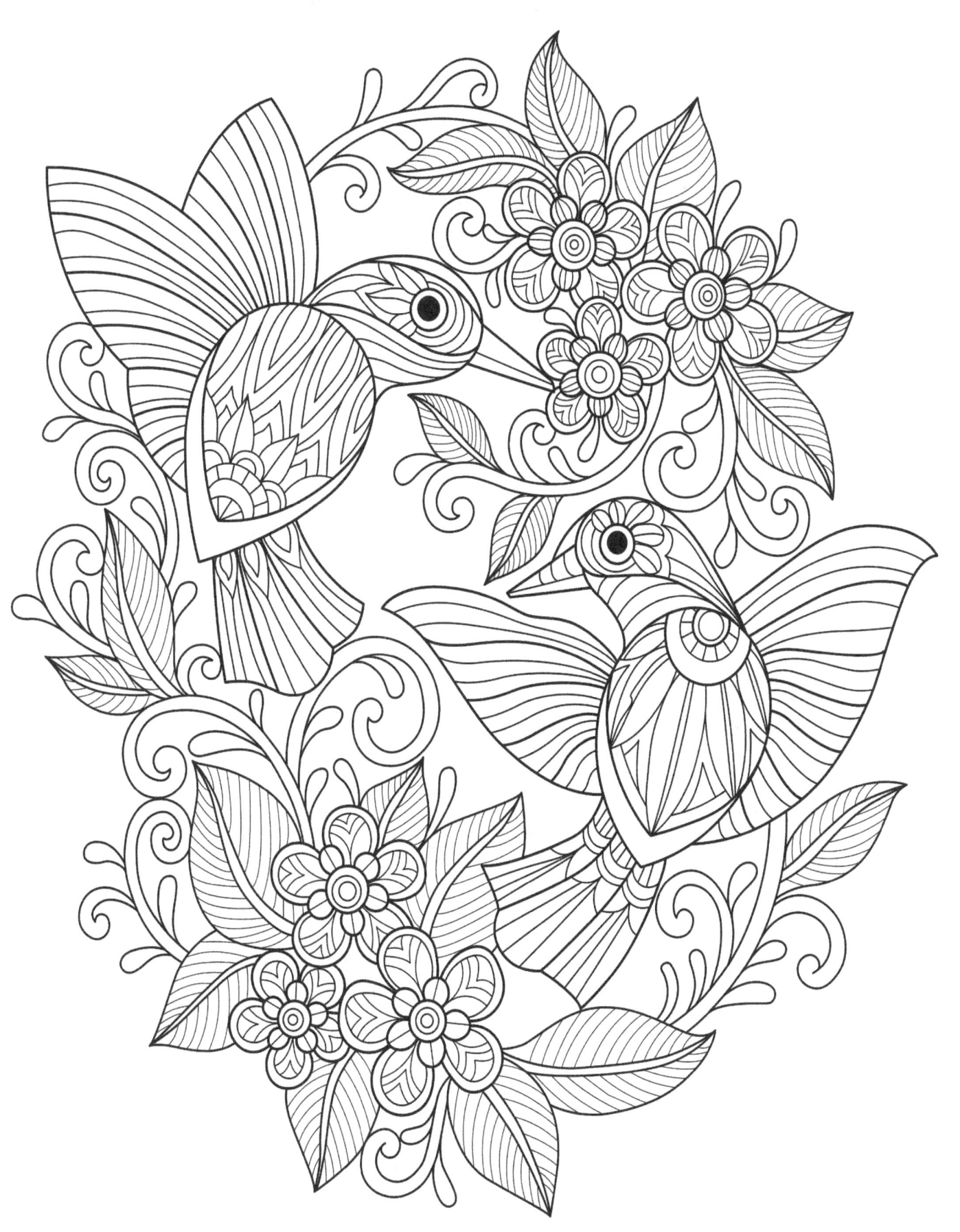

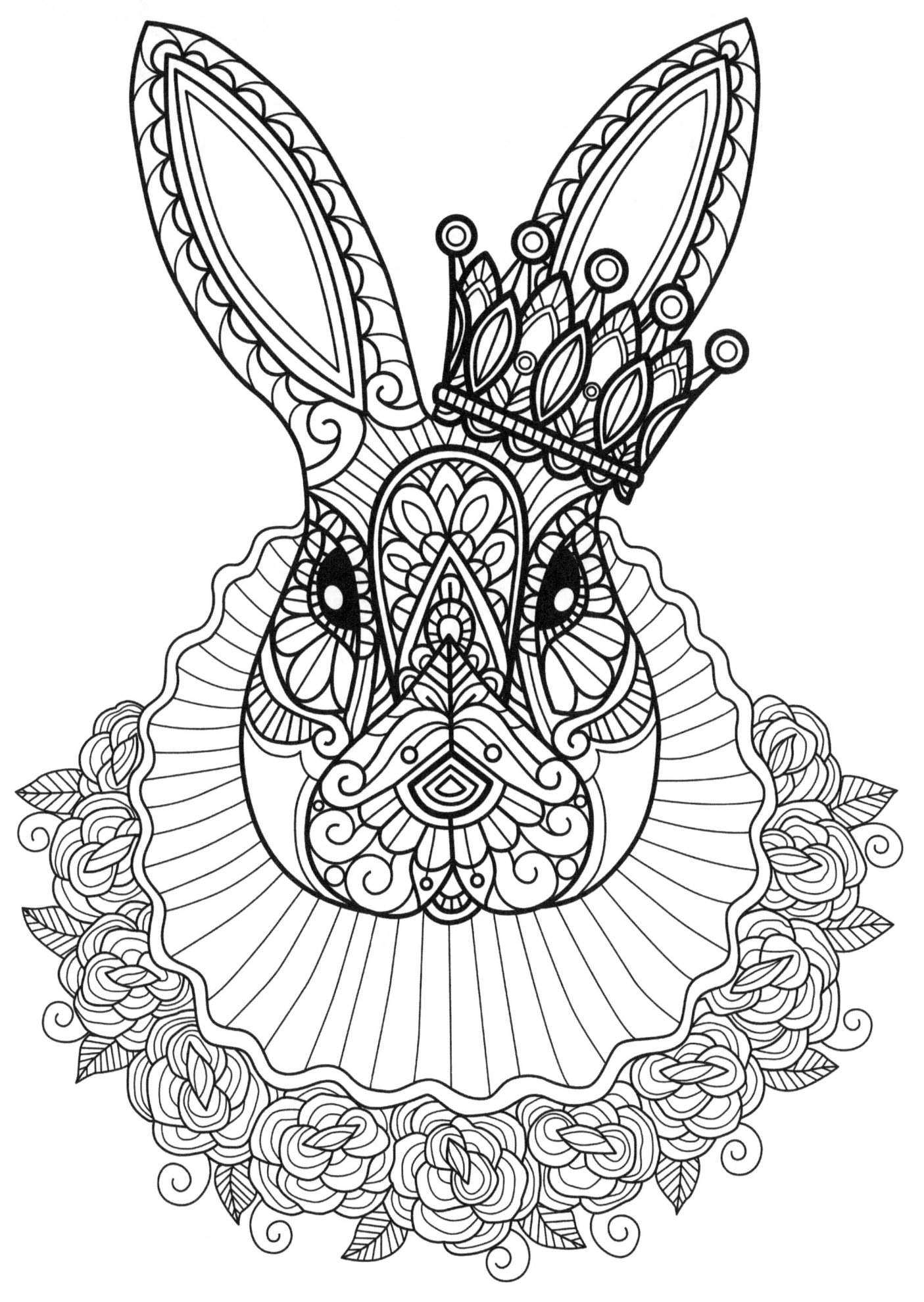

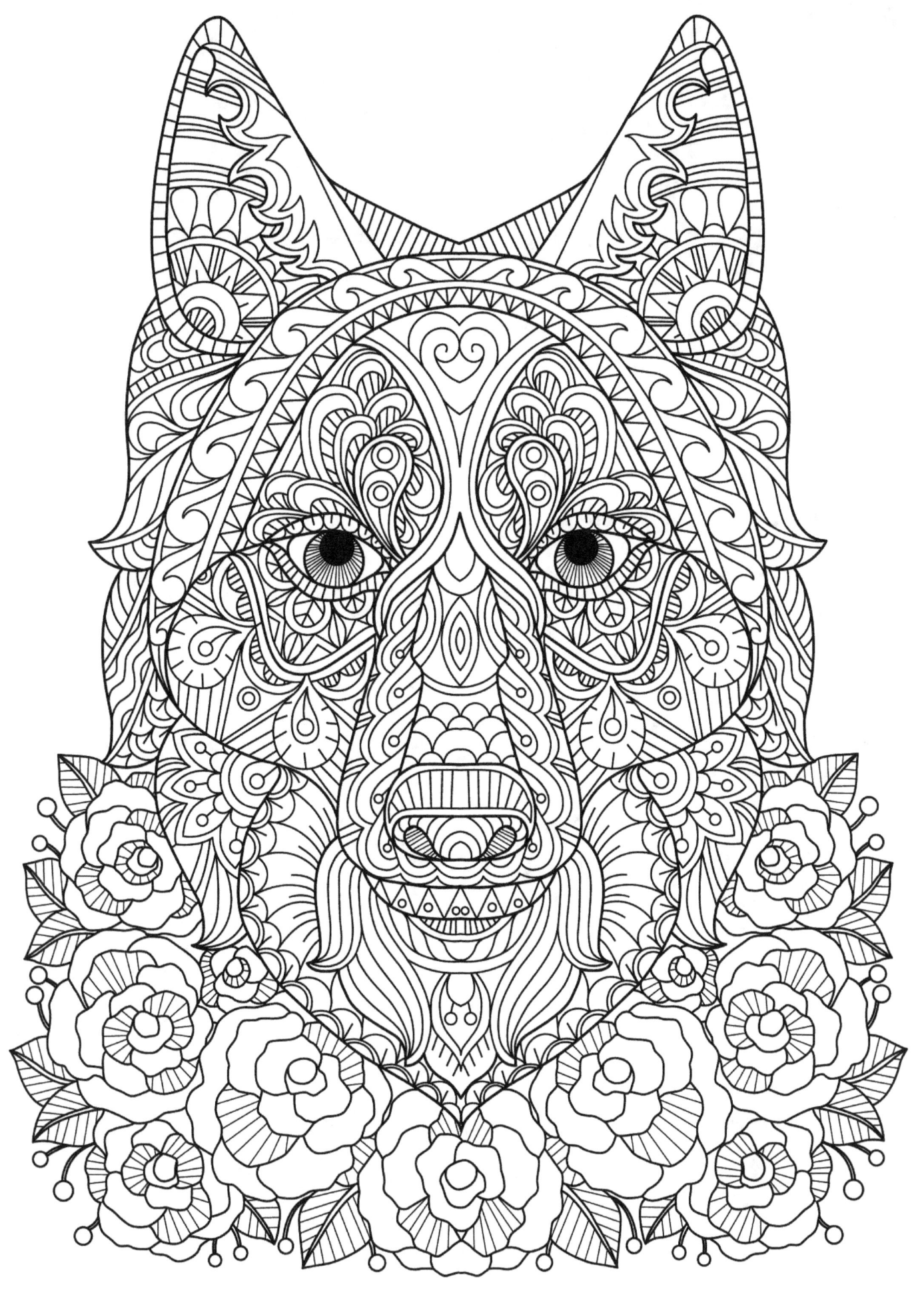

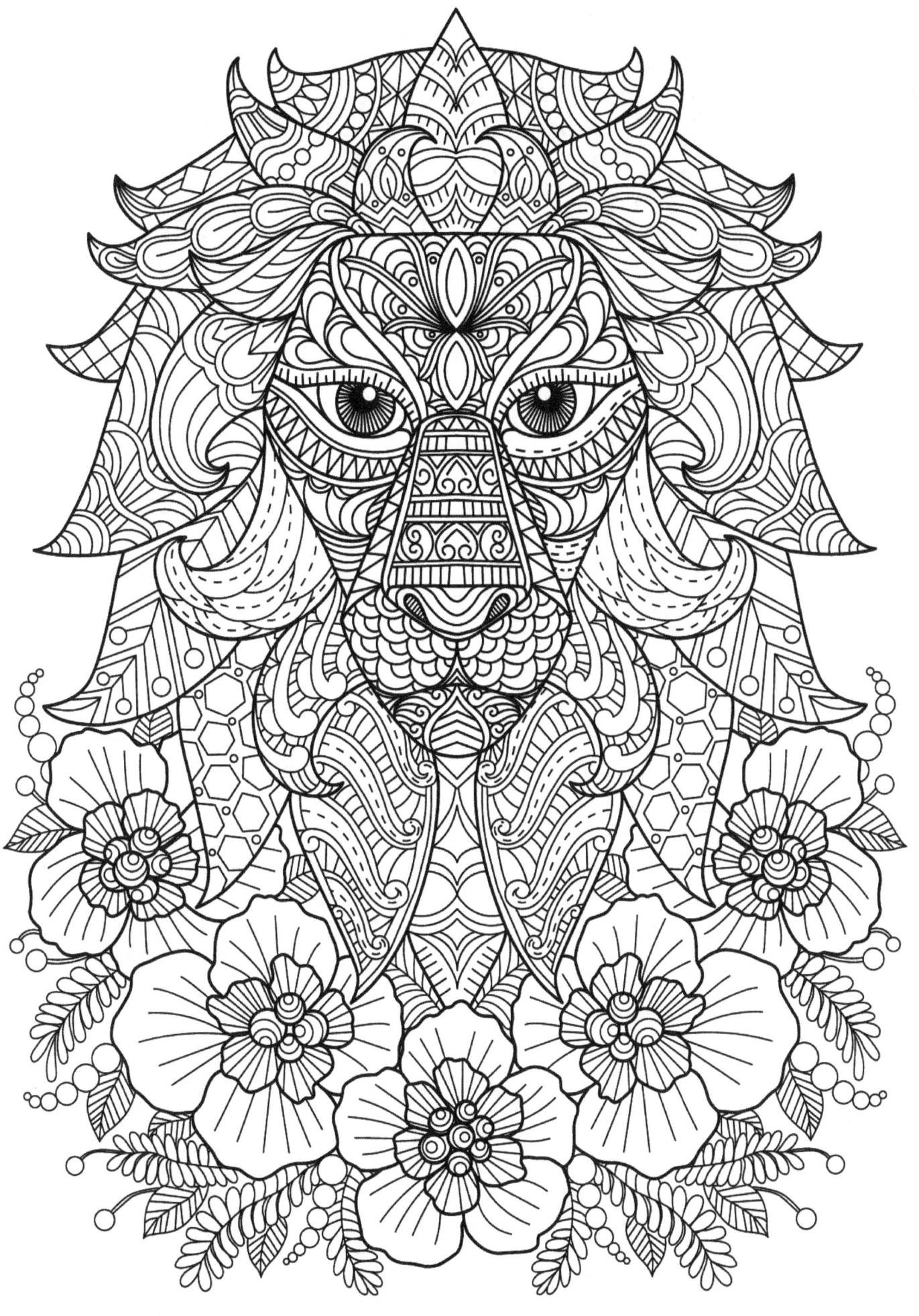

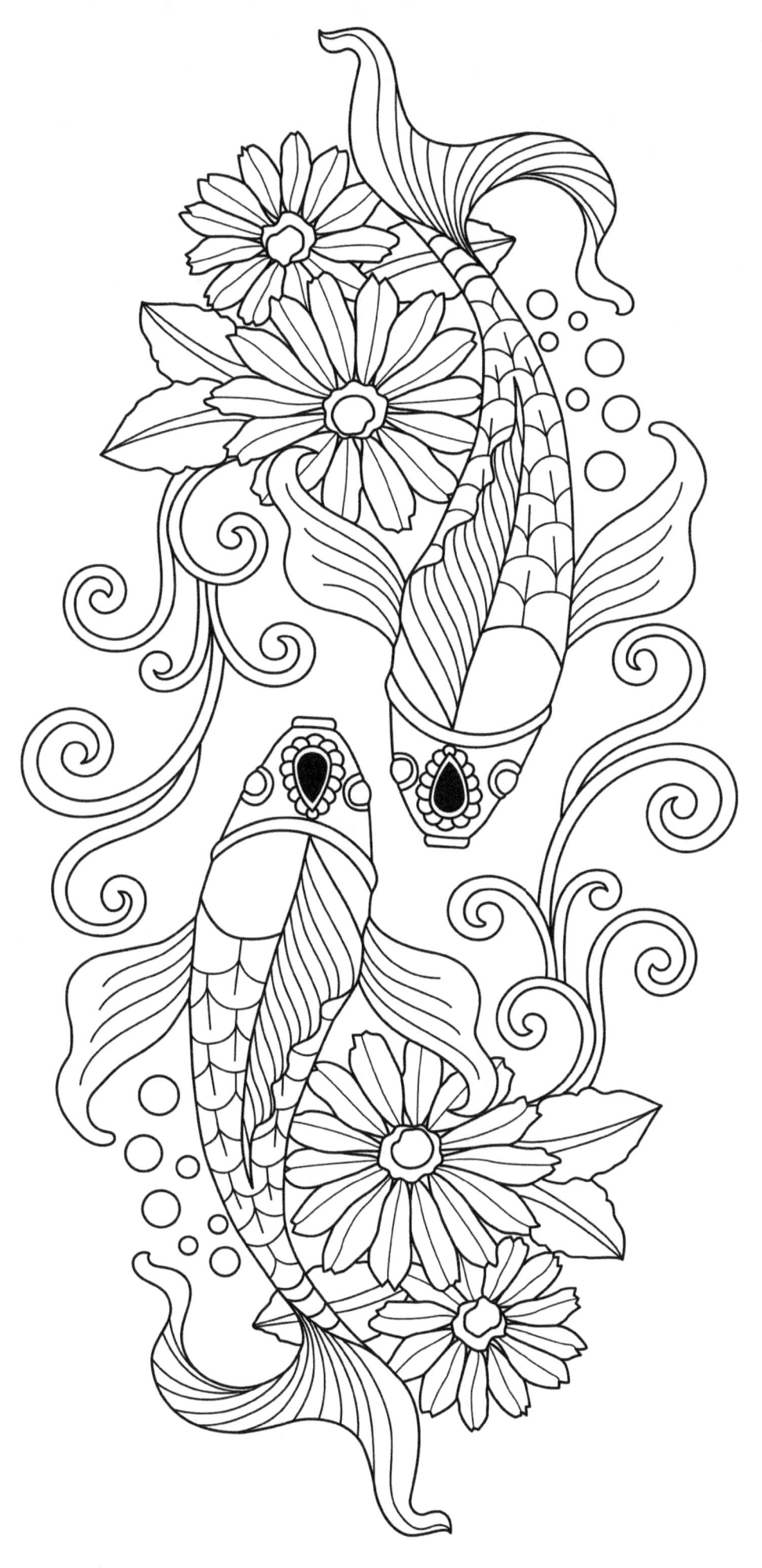

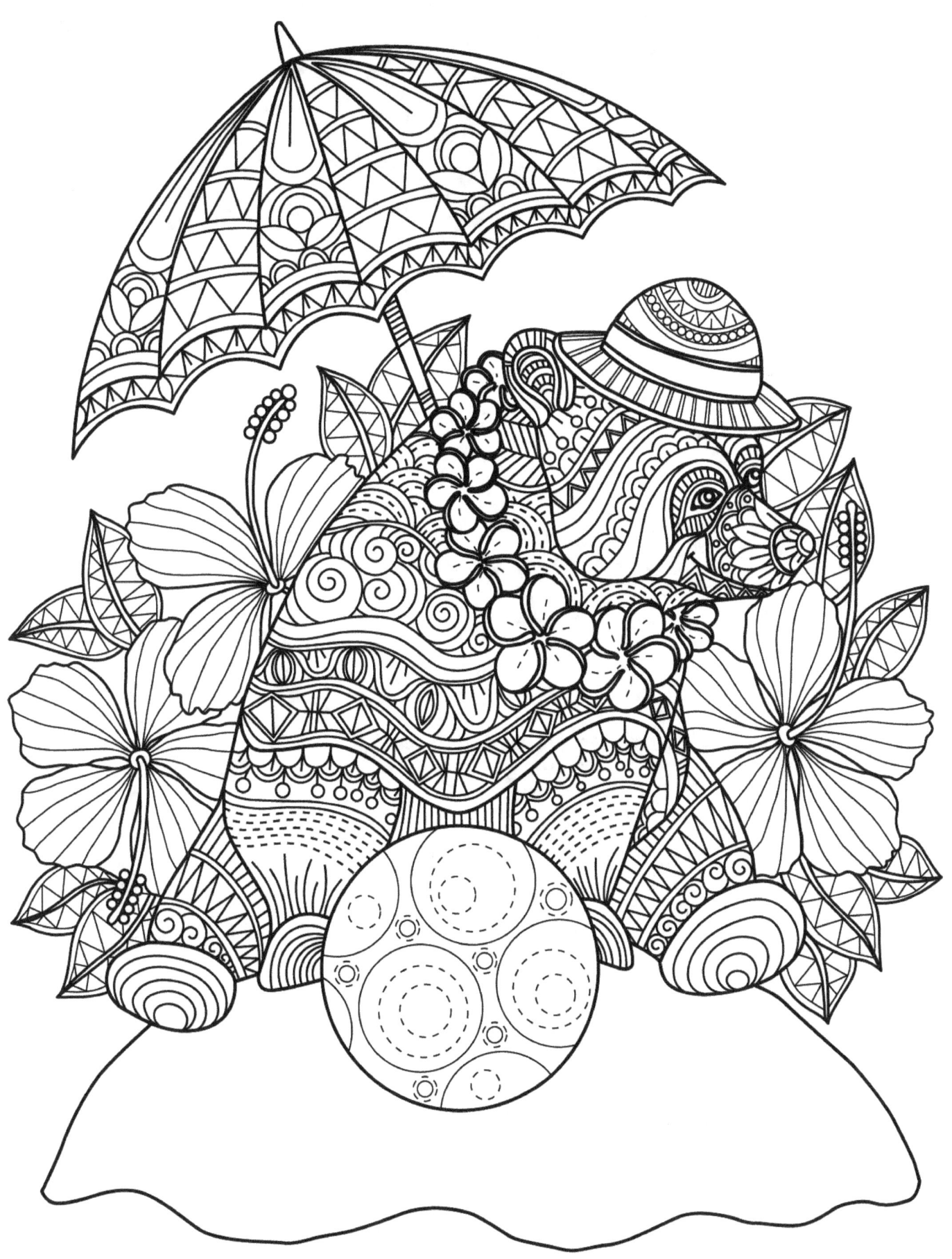

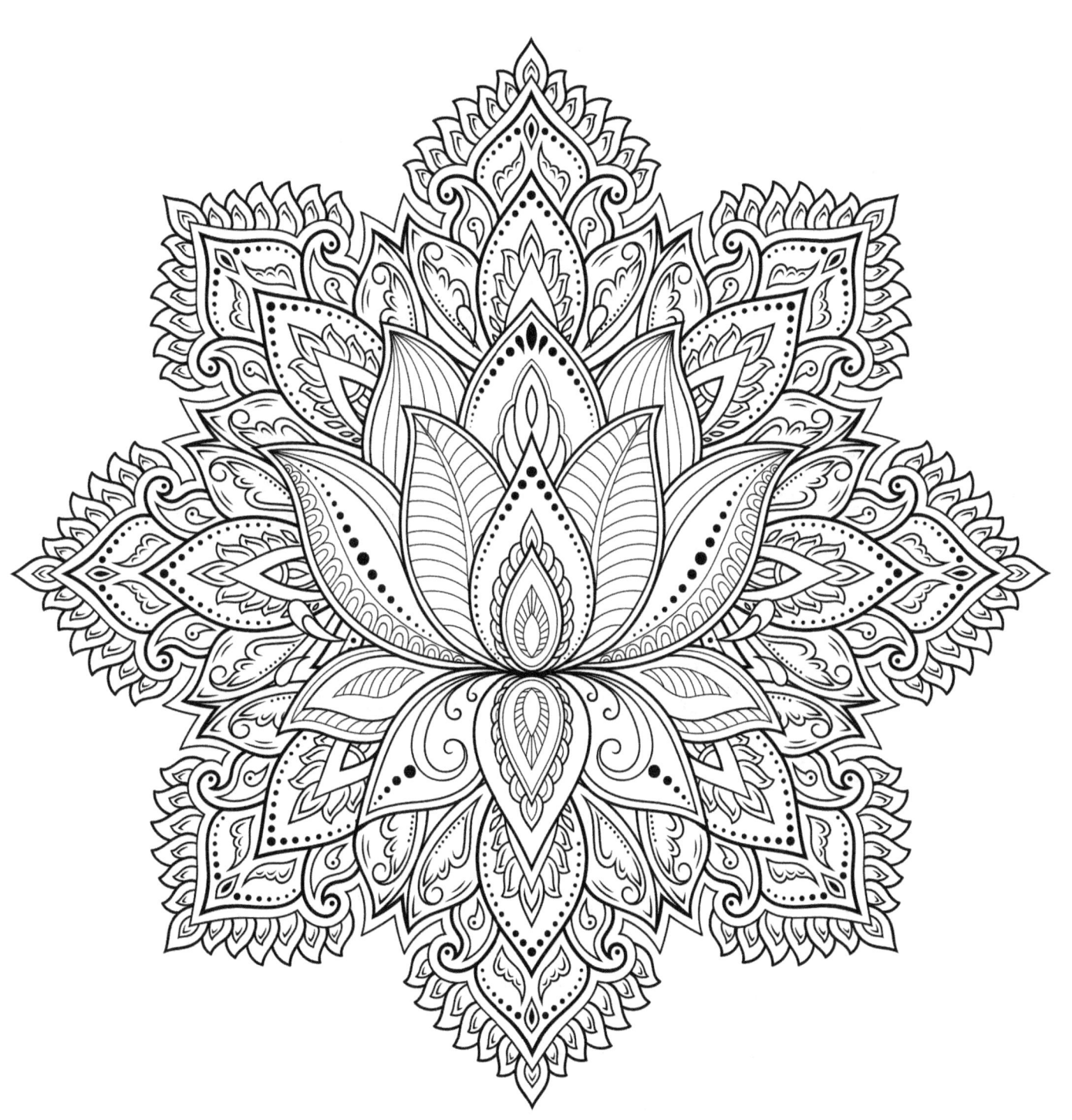

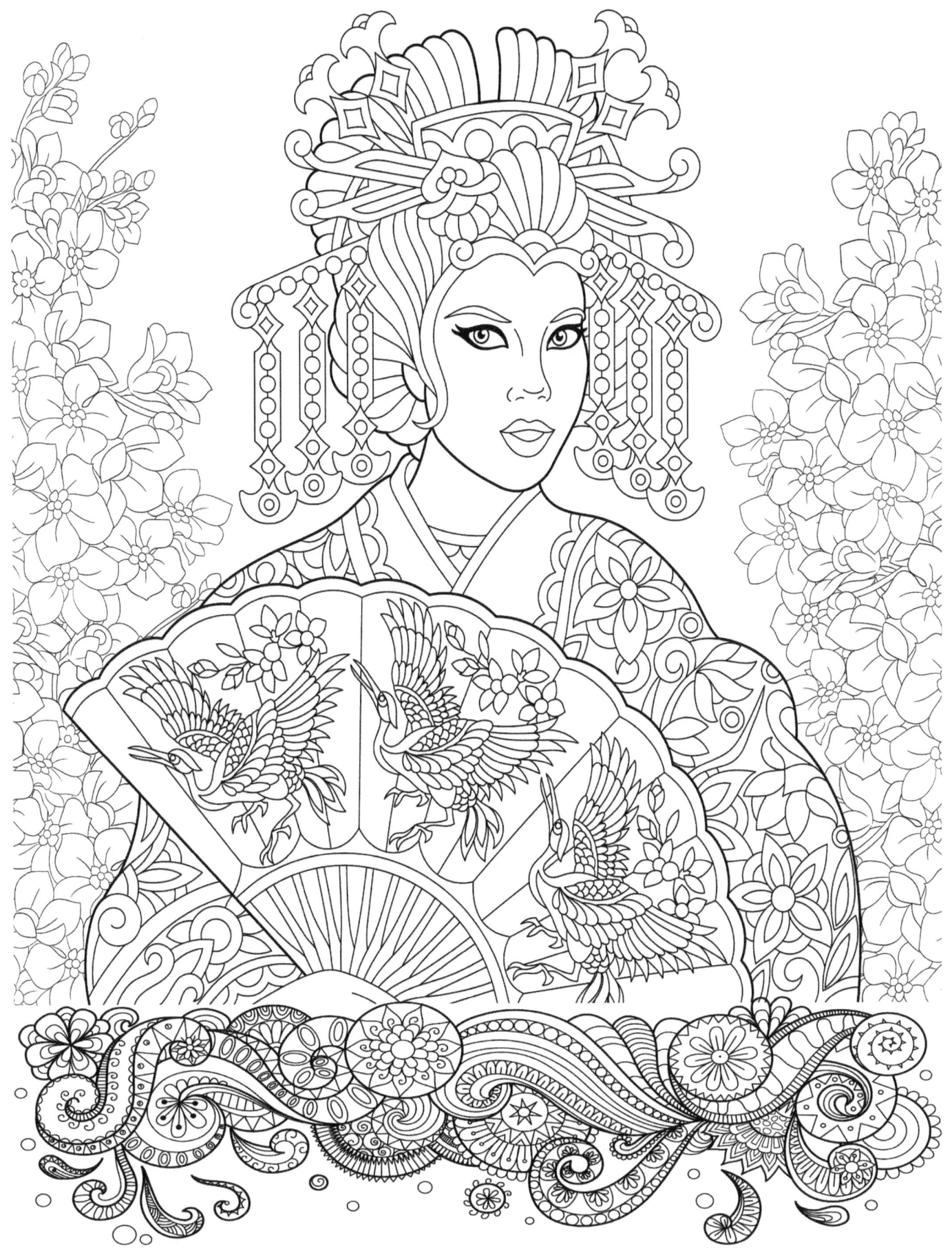

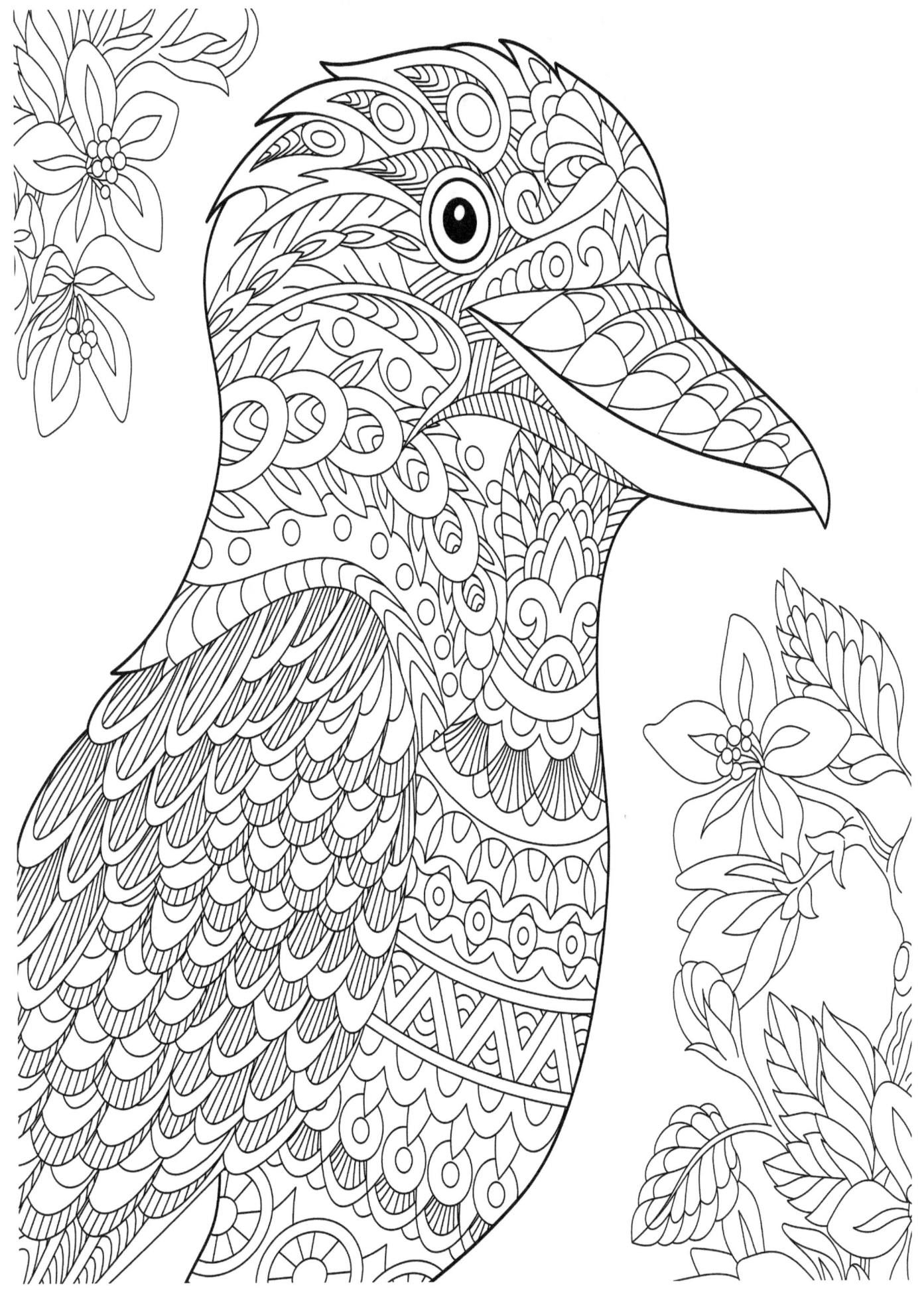

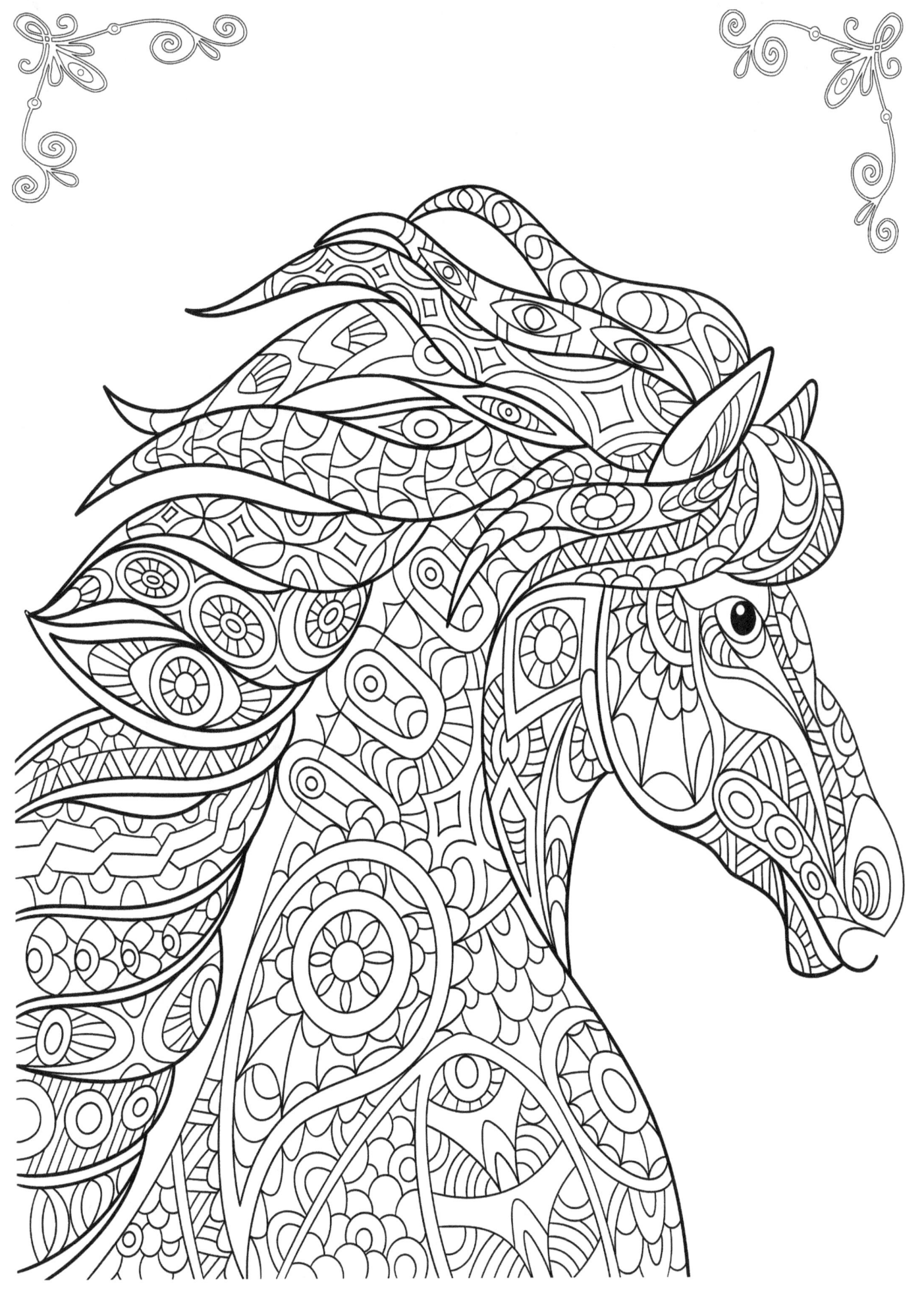

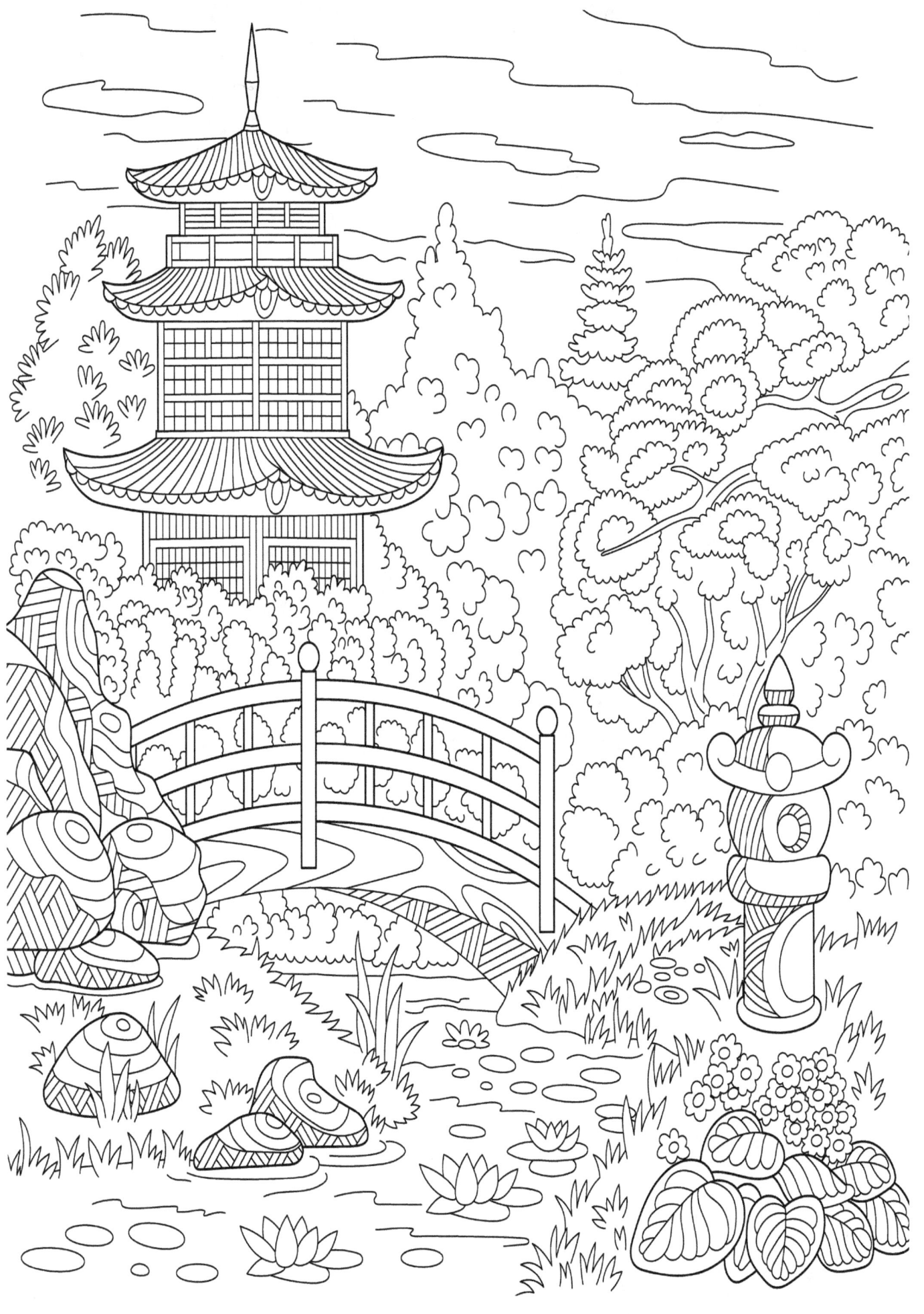

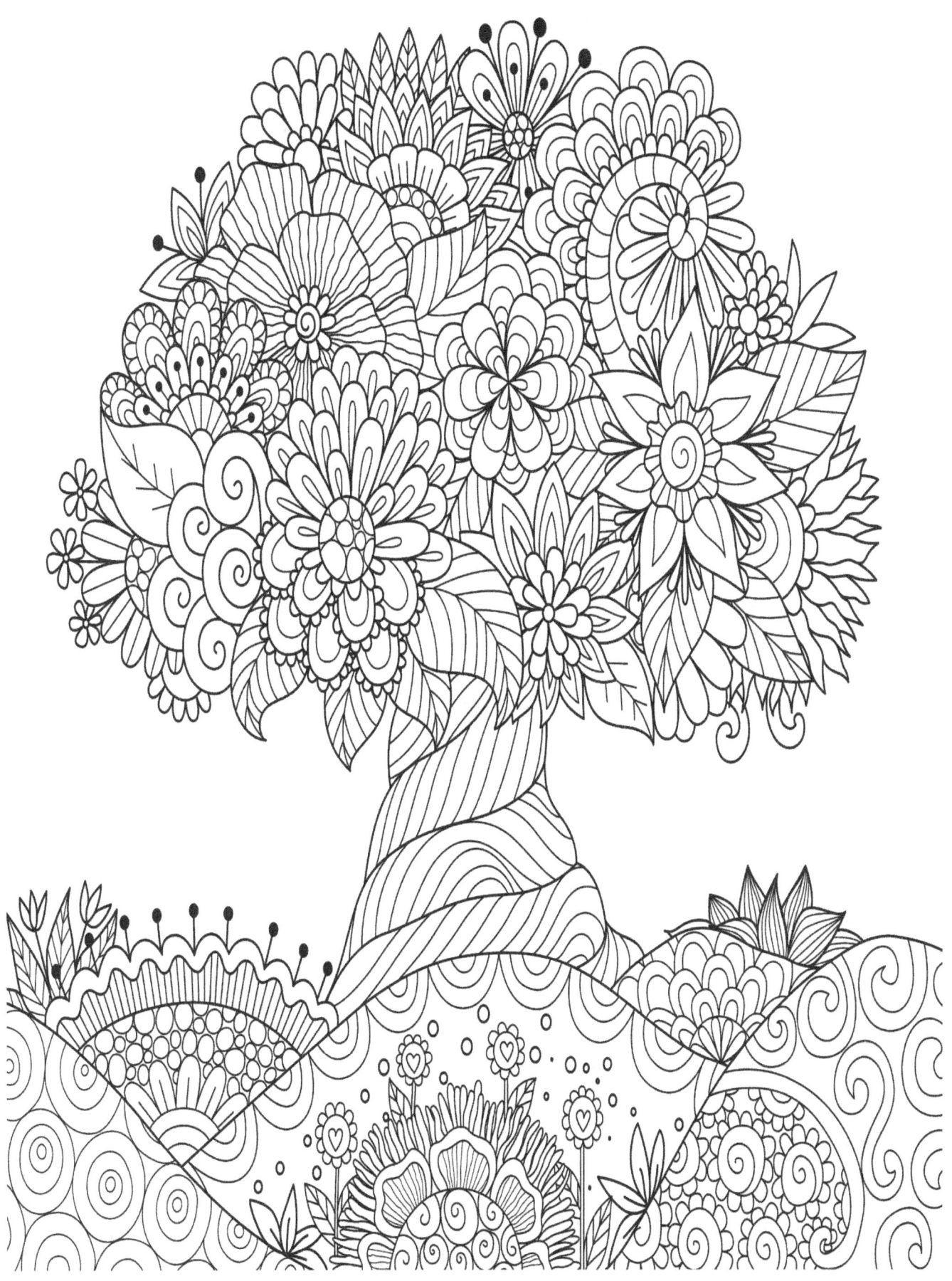

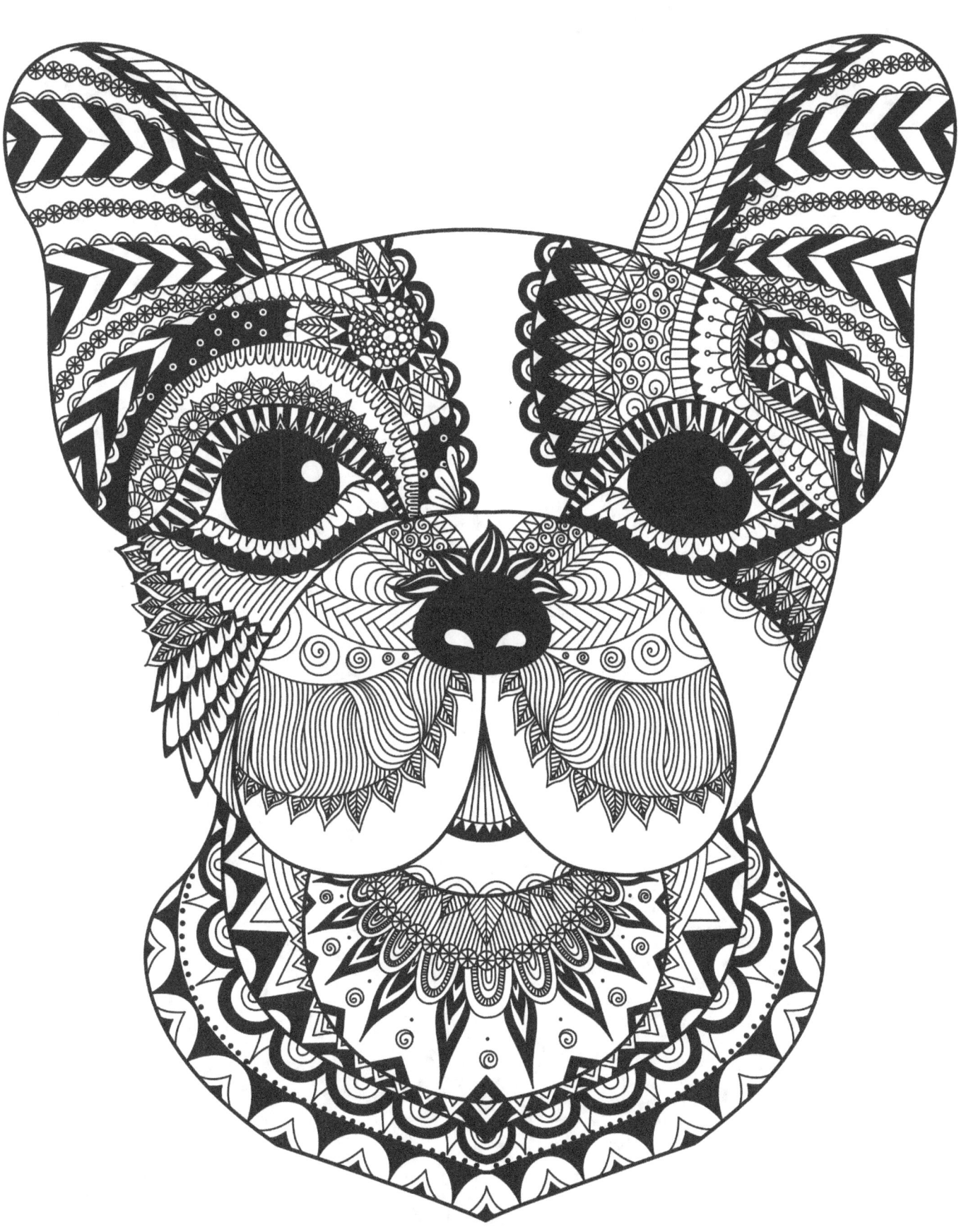

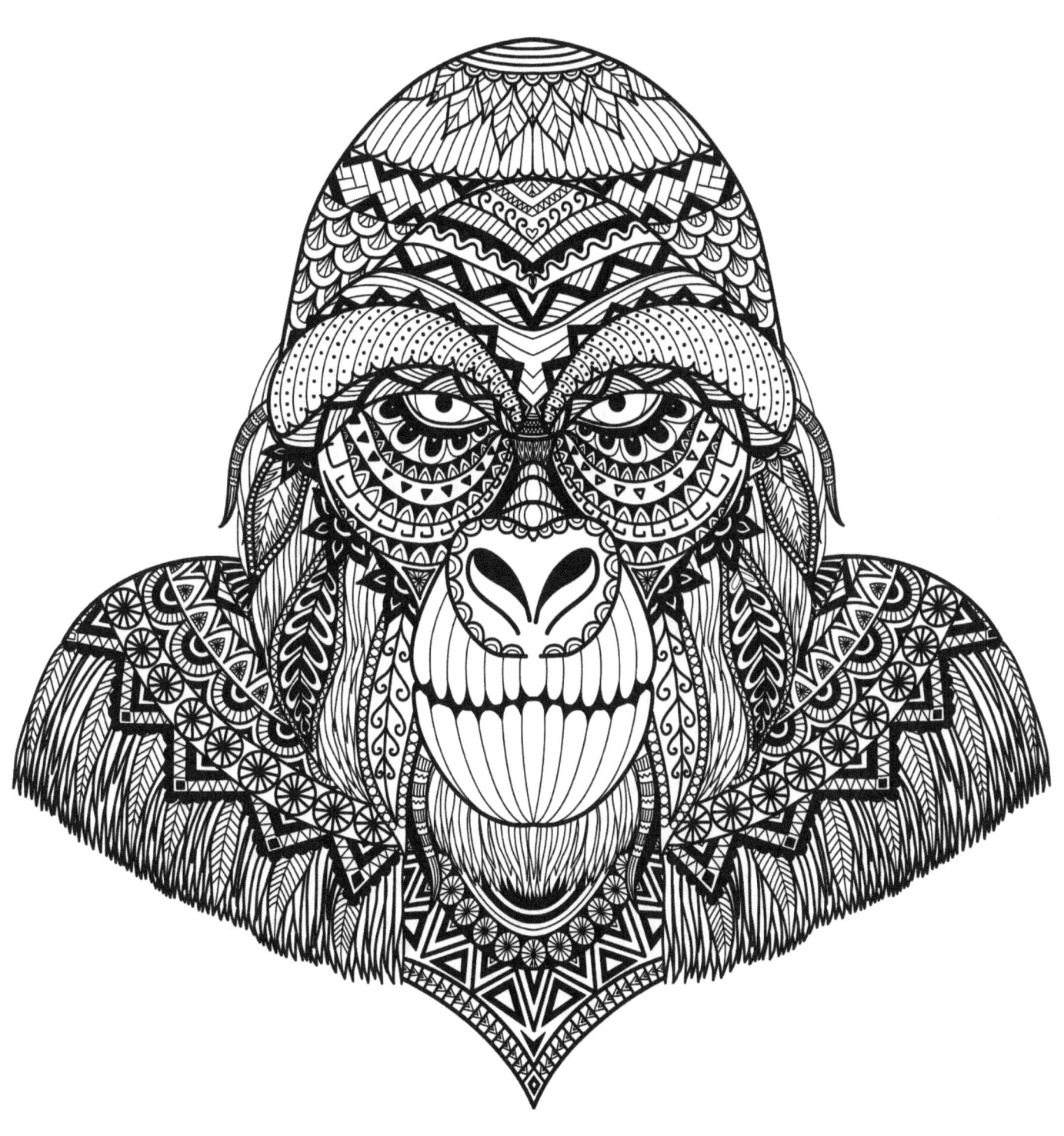

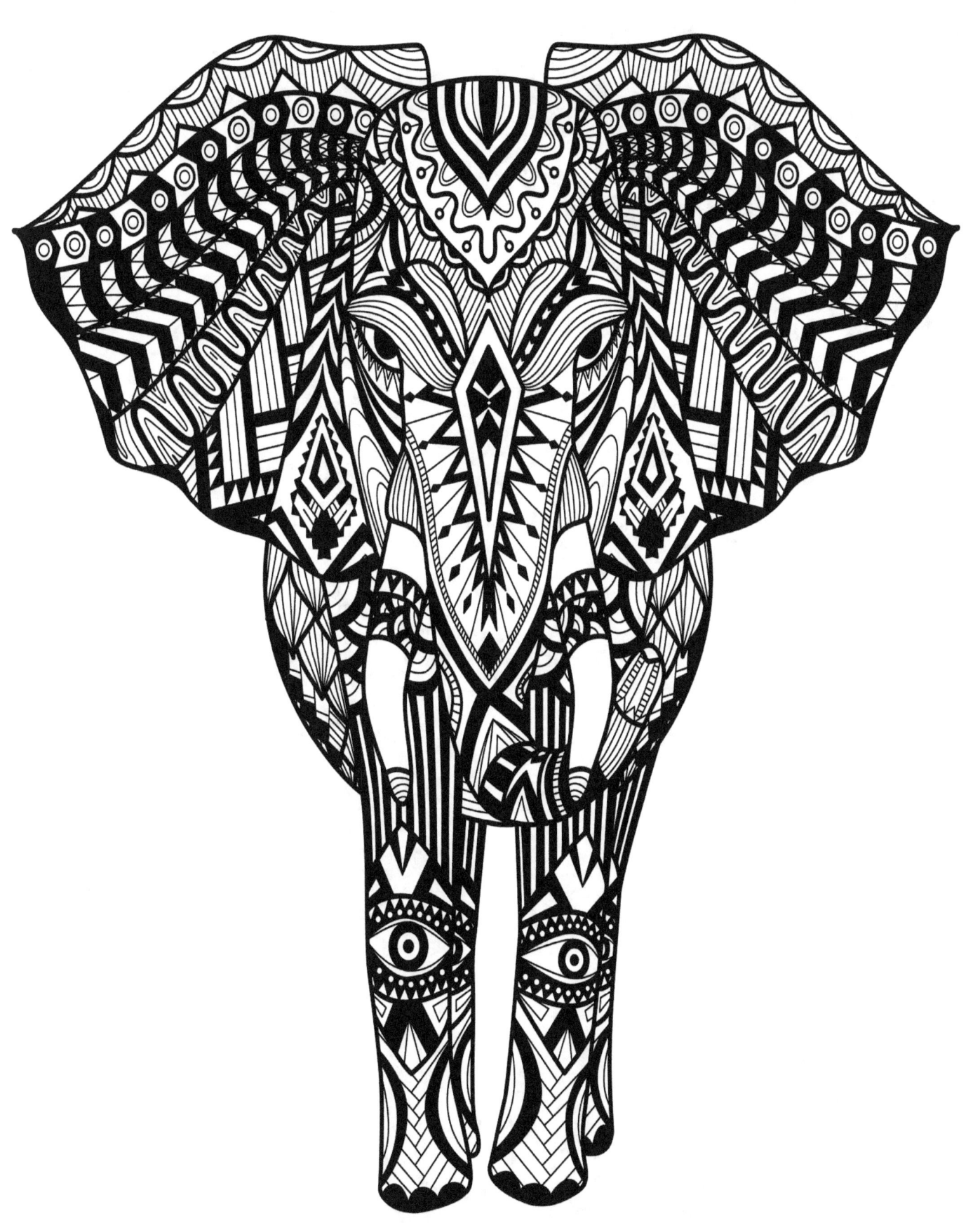

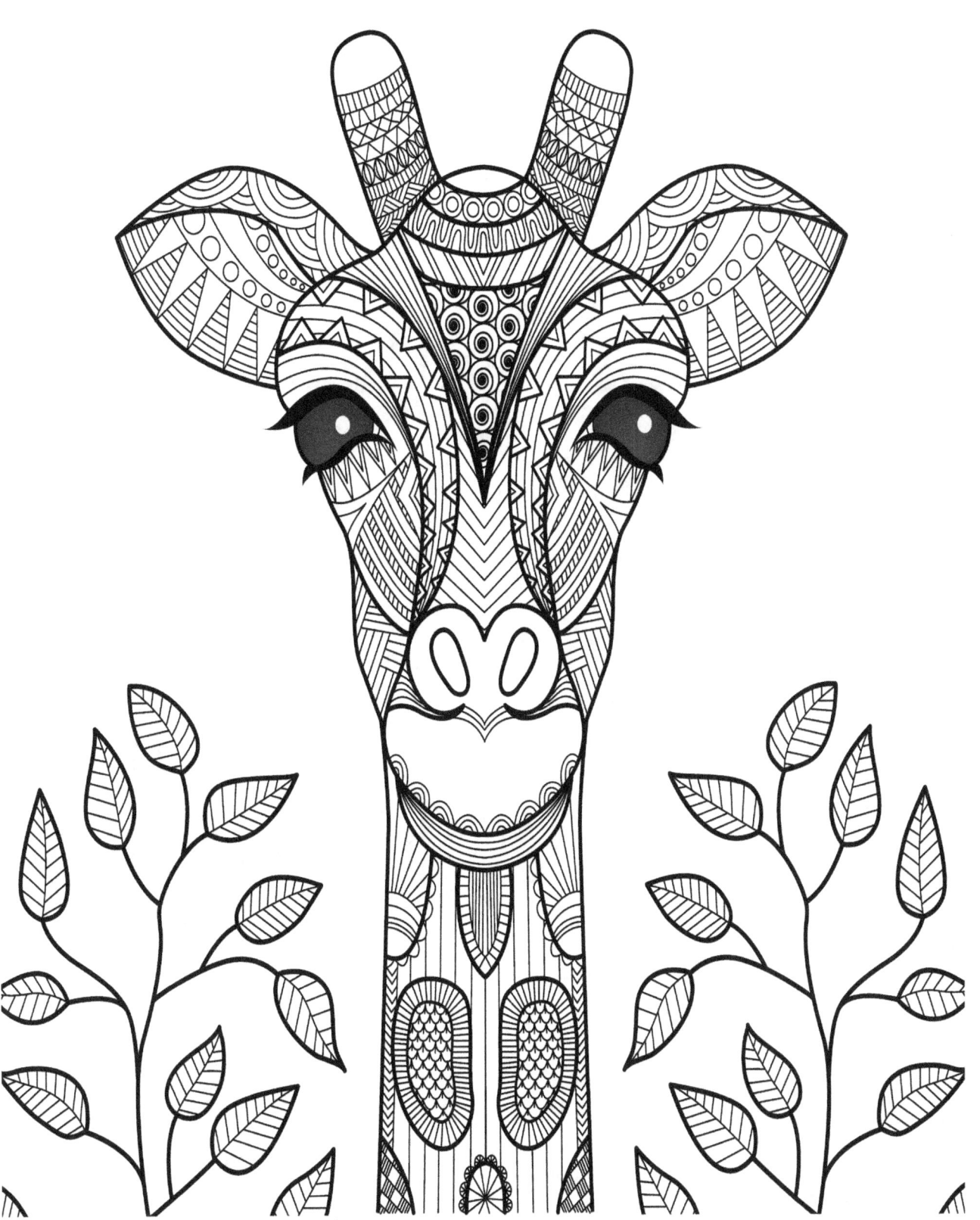

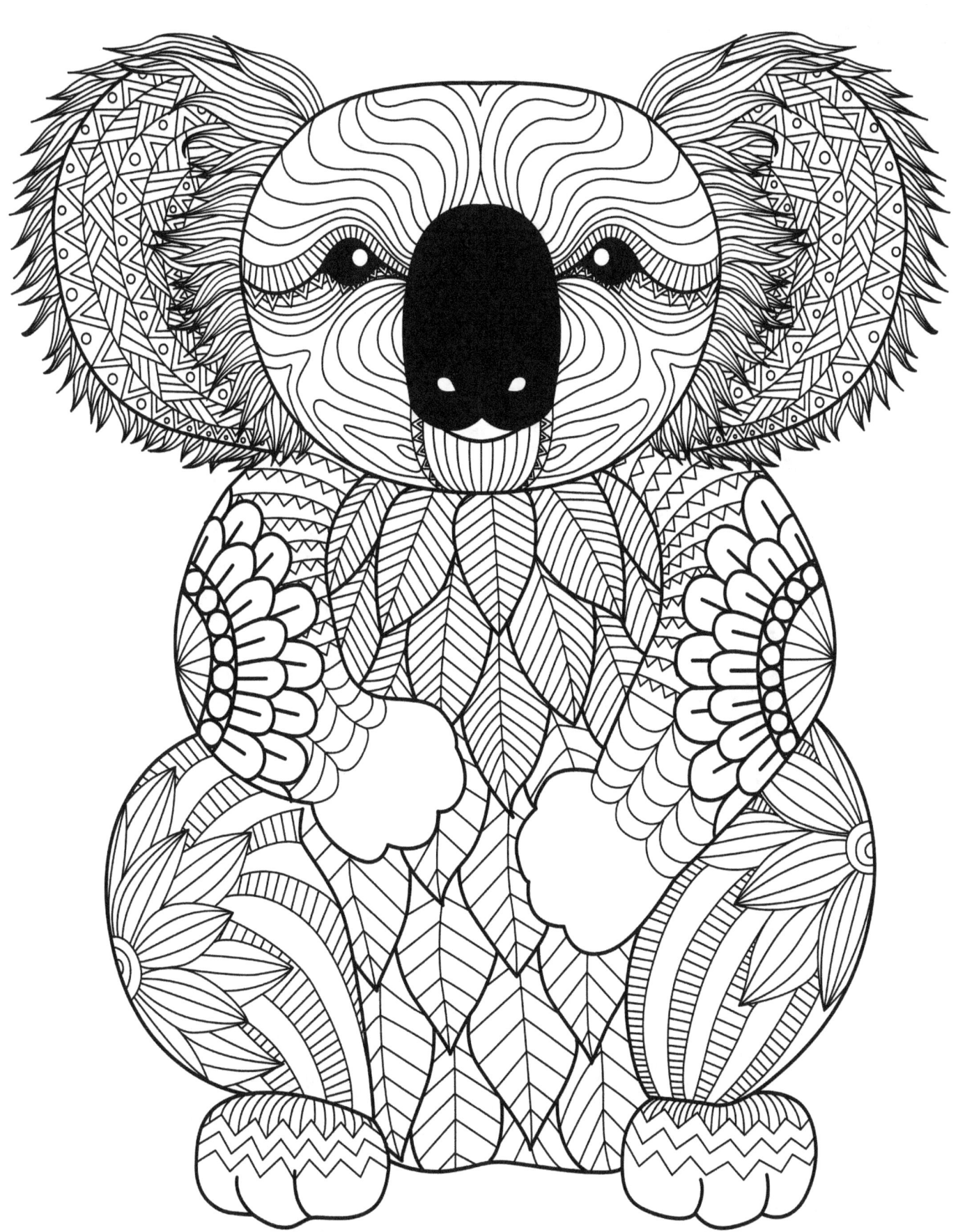

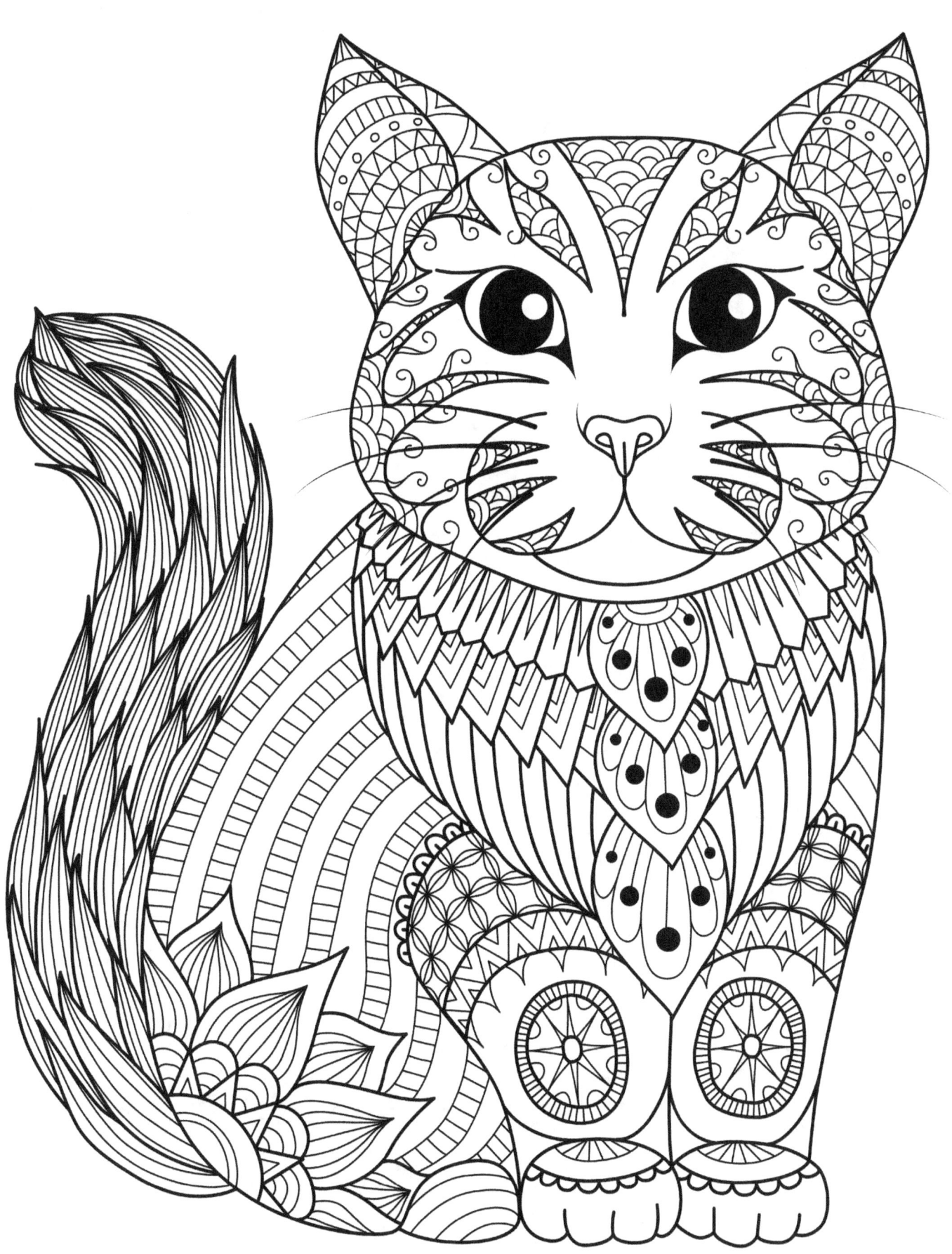

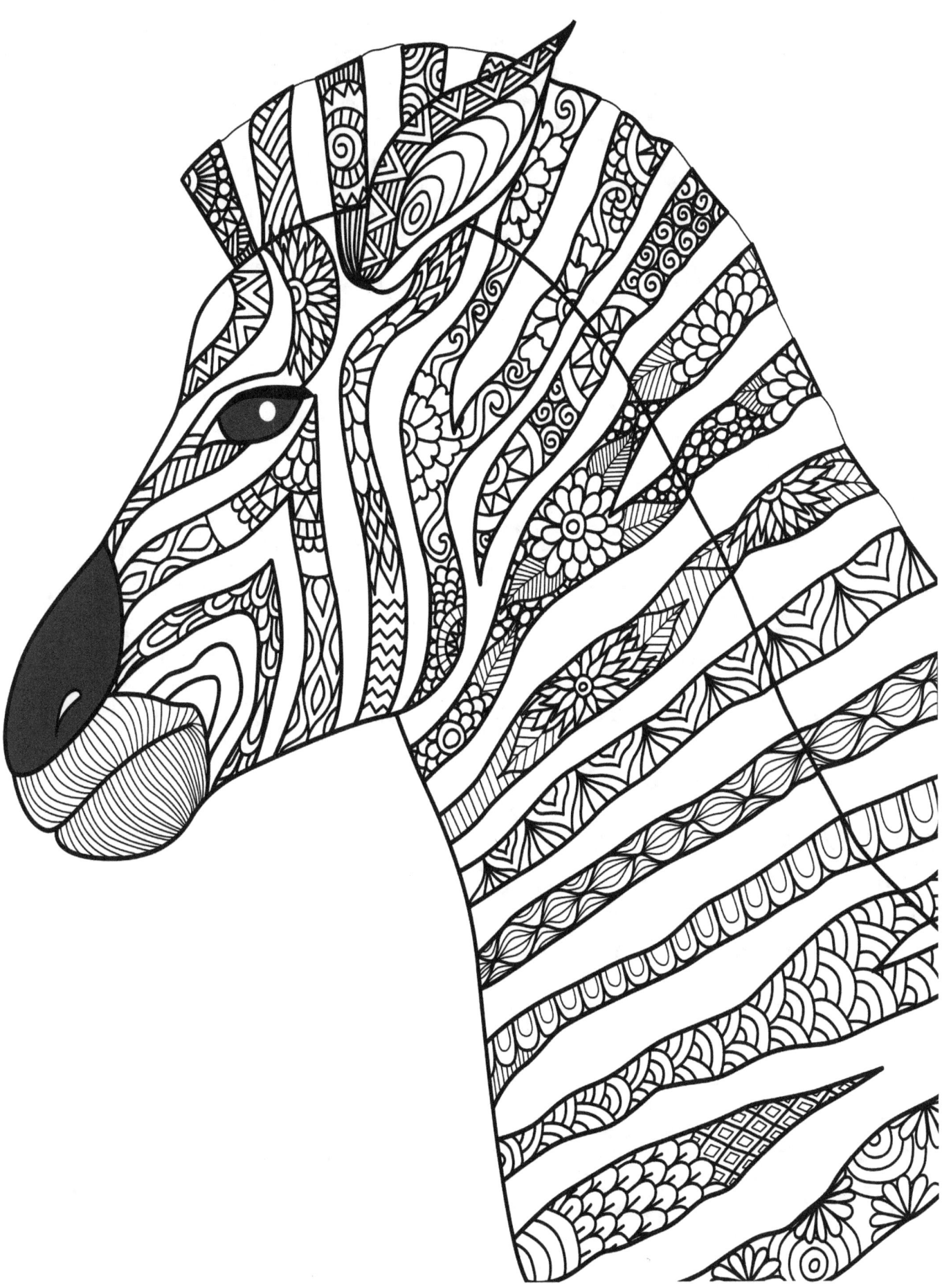

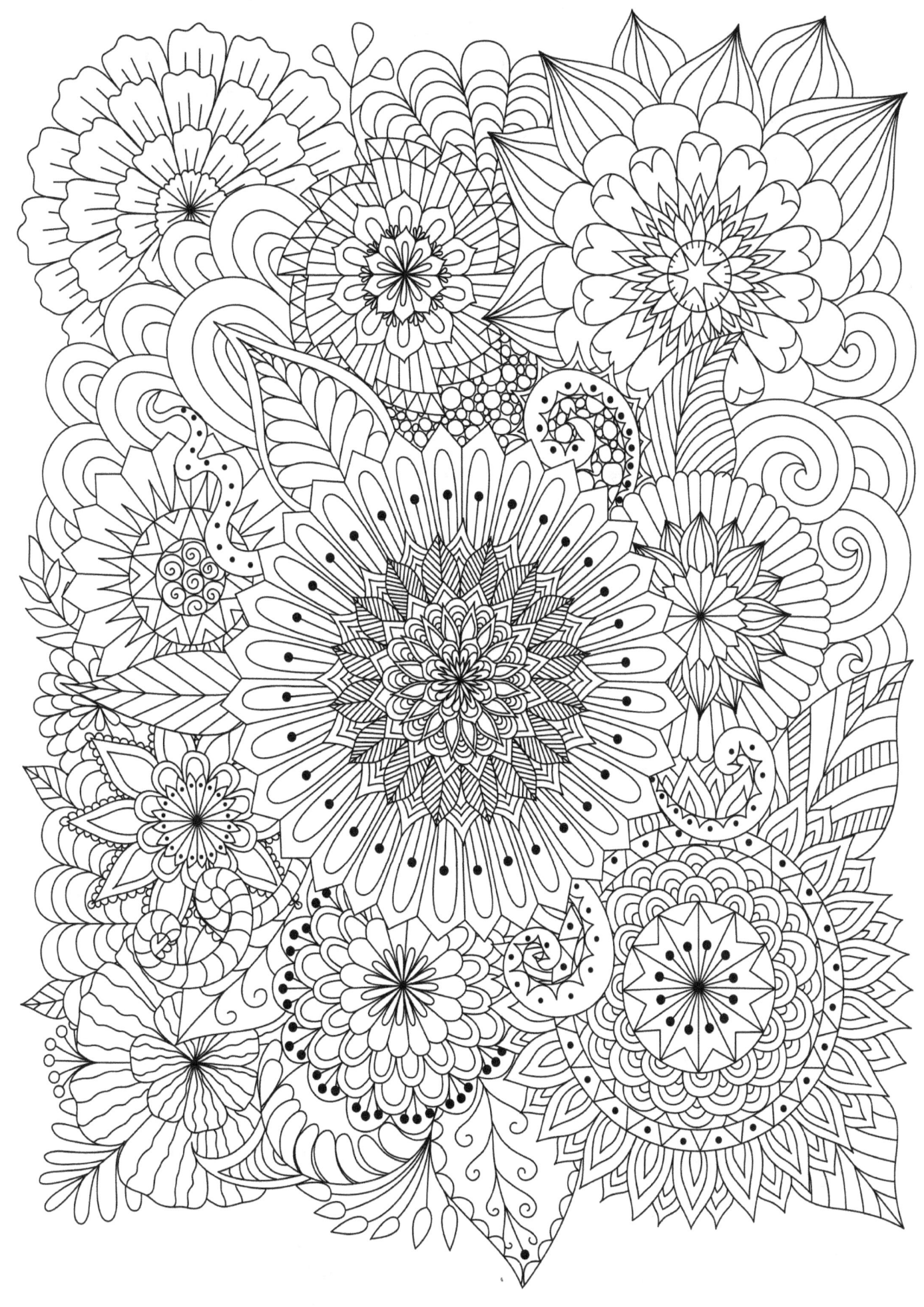

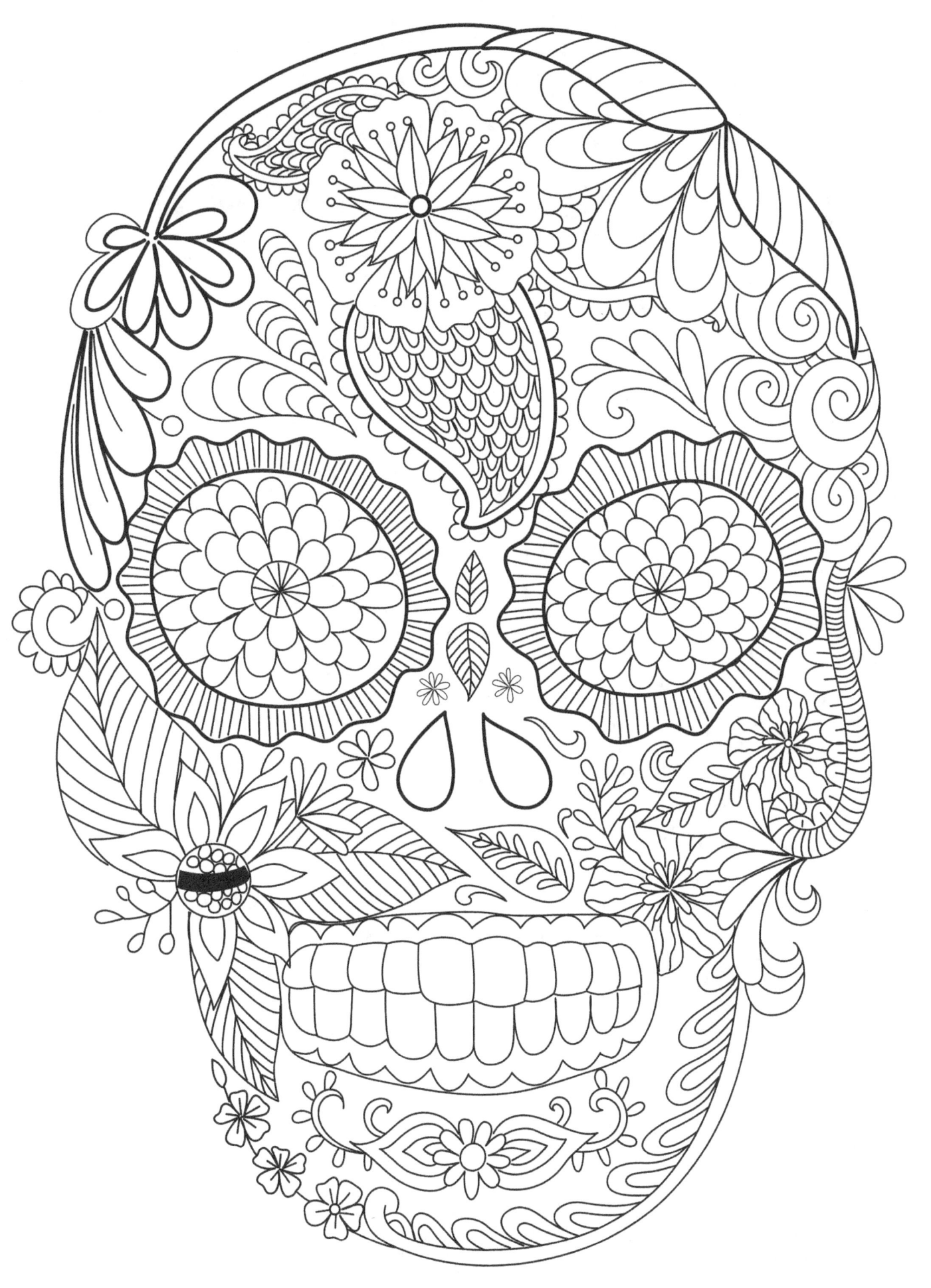

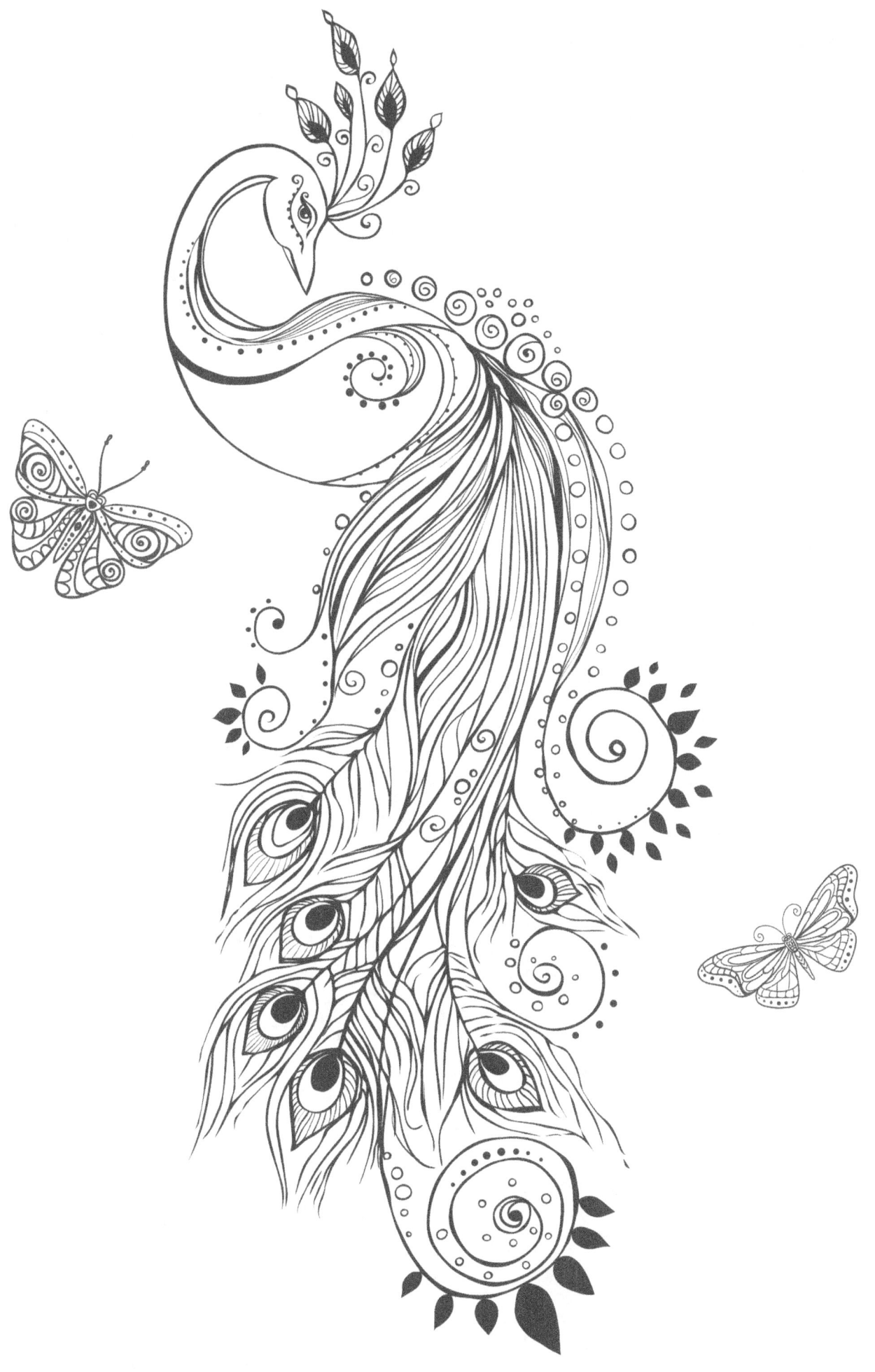

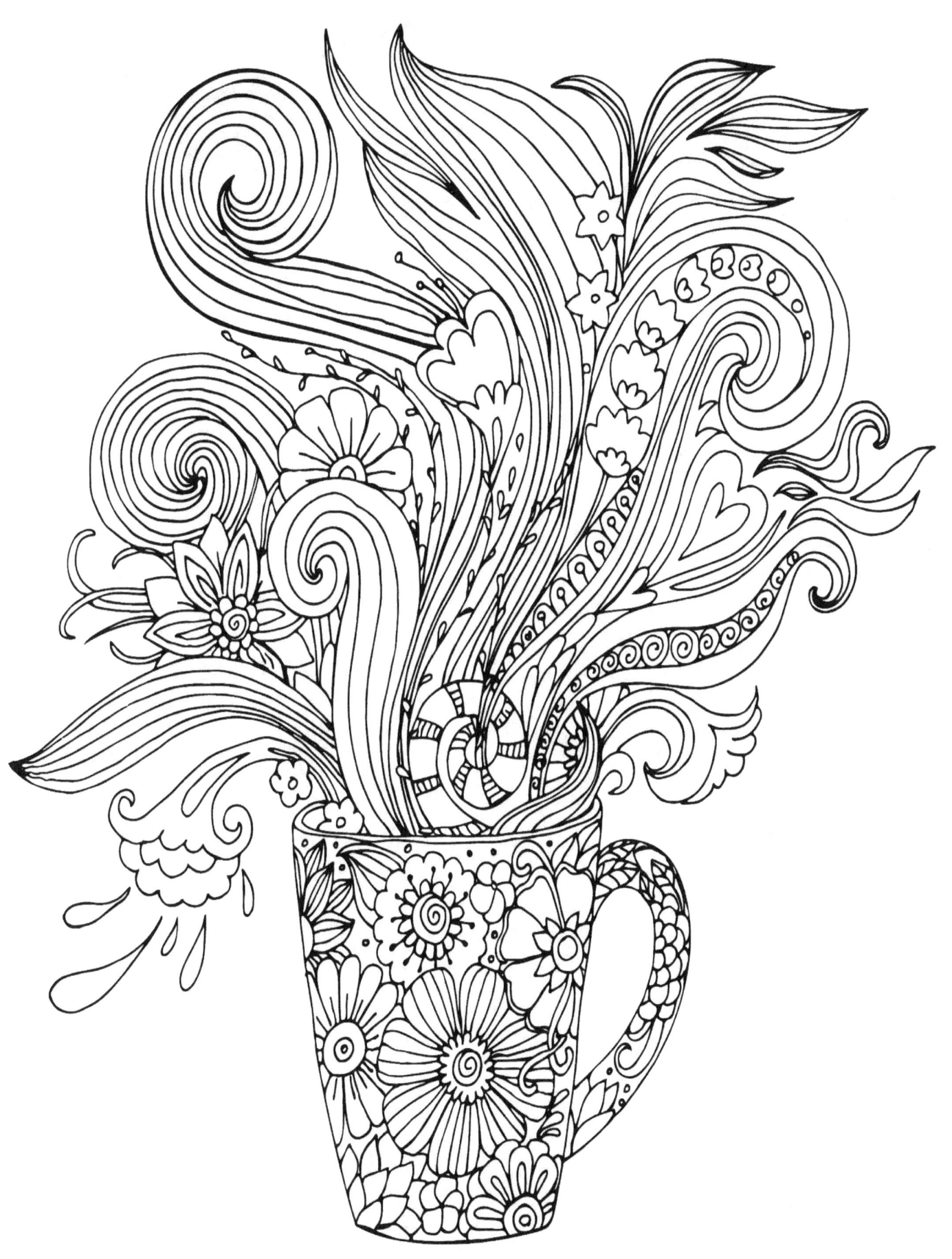

# Bonus Section!

The following eleven images were drawn on paper and then turned into digital images.

Although not as crisp as the other images in this book, we like to think they have a certain charm!

We hope you enjoy them!

# Hoary Shrubby Stock

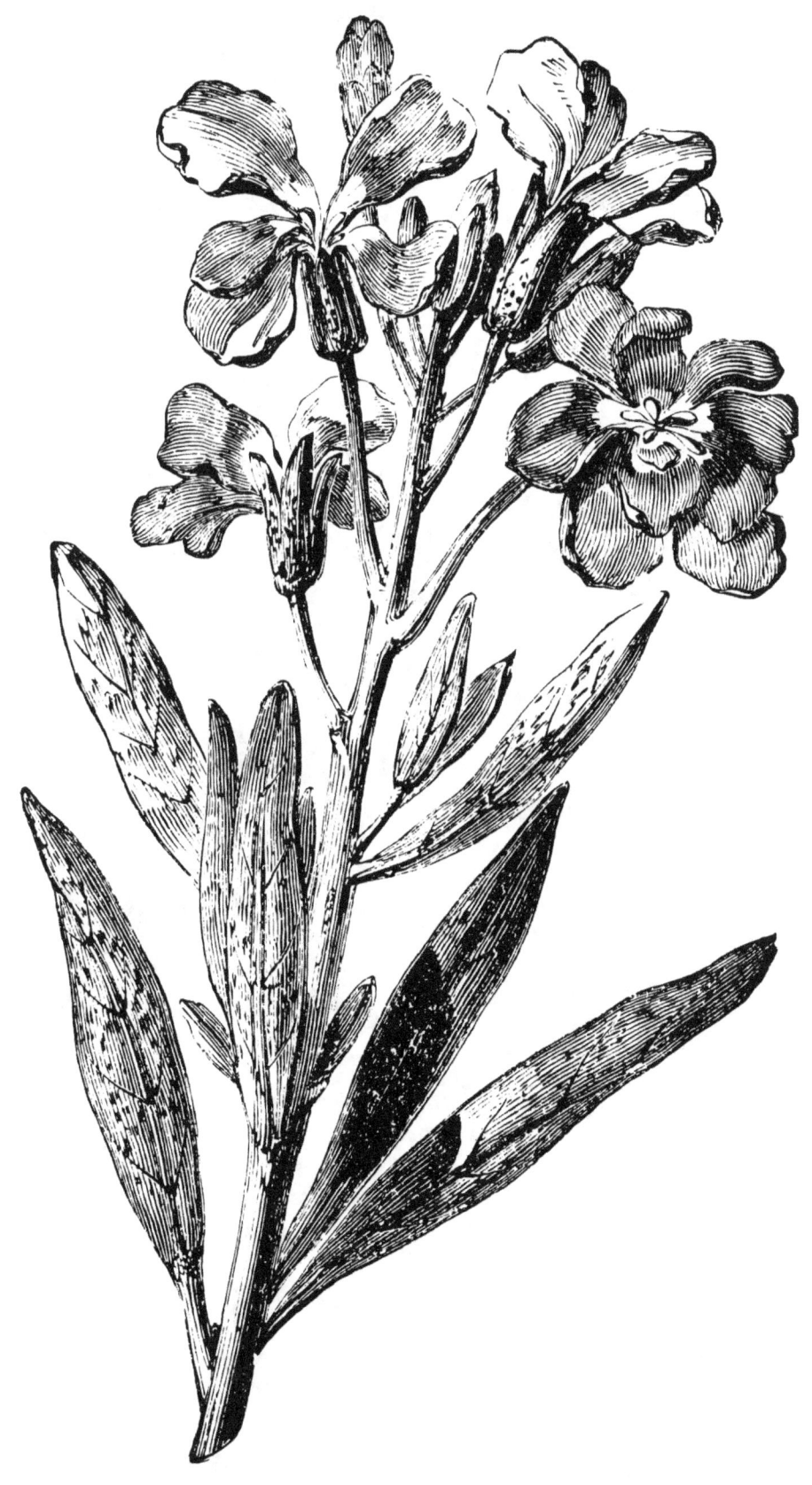

# Honeysuckle

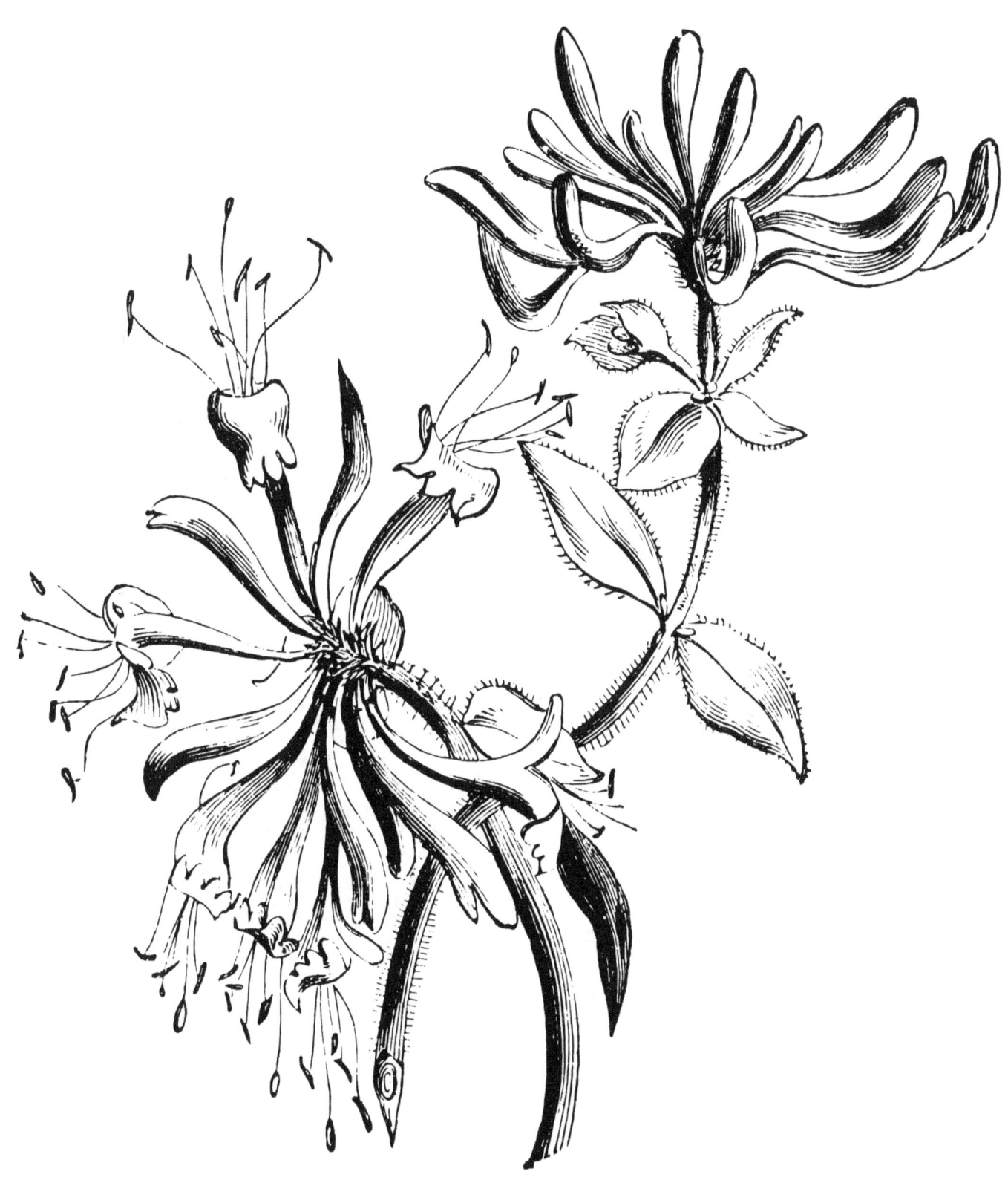

# Burnet-Leaved Rose

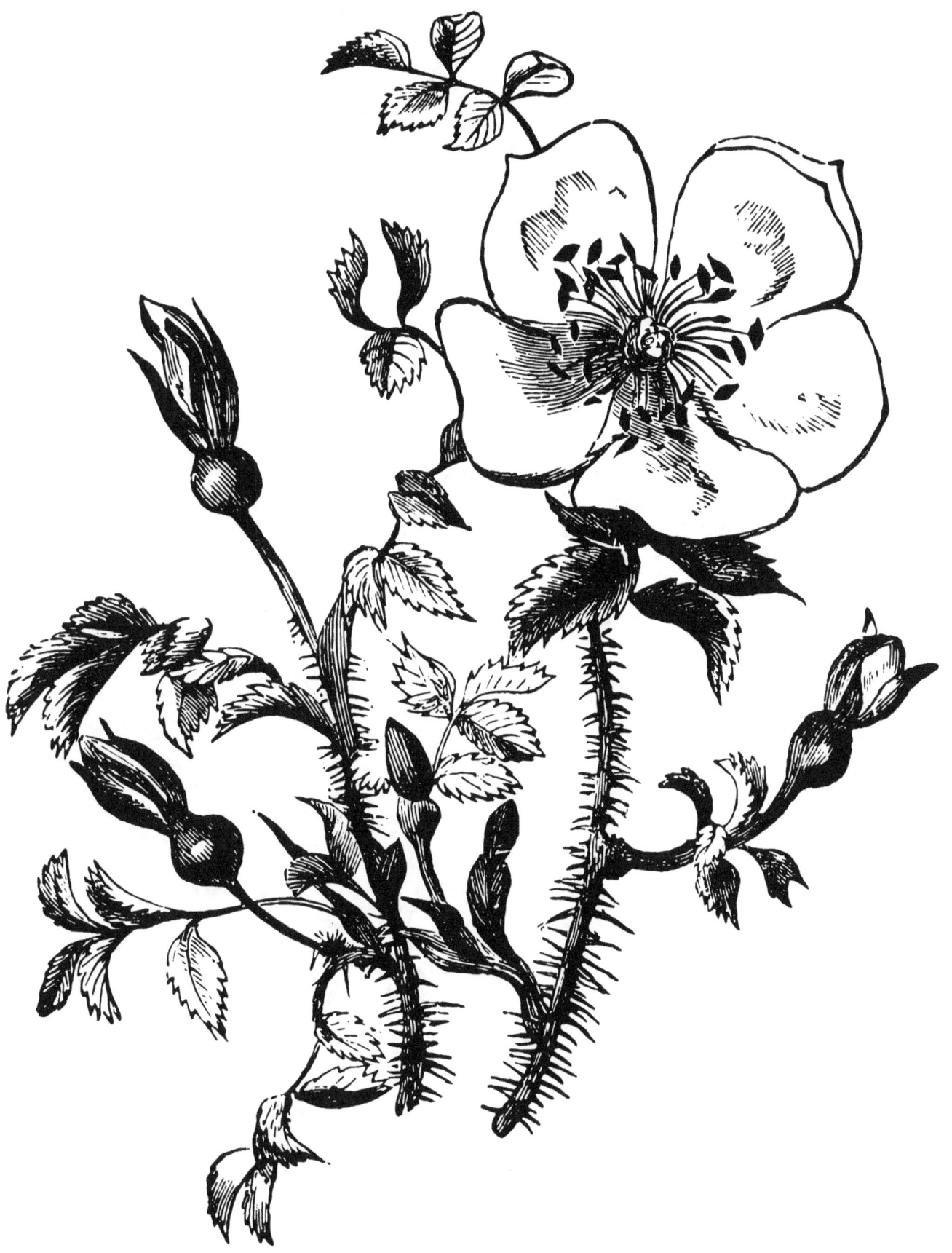

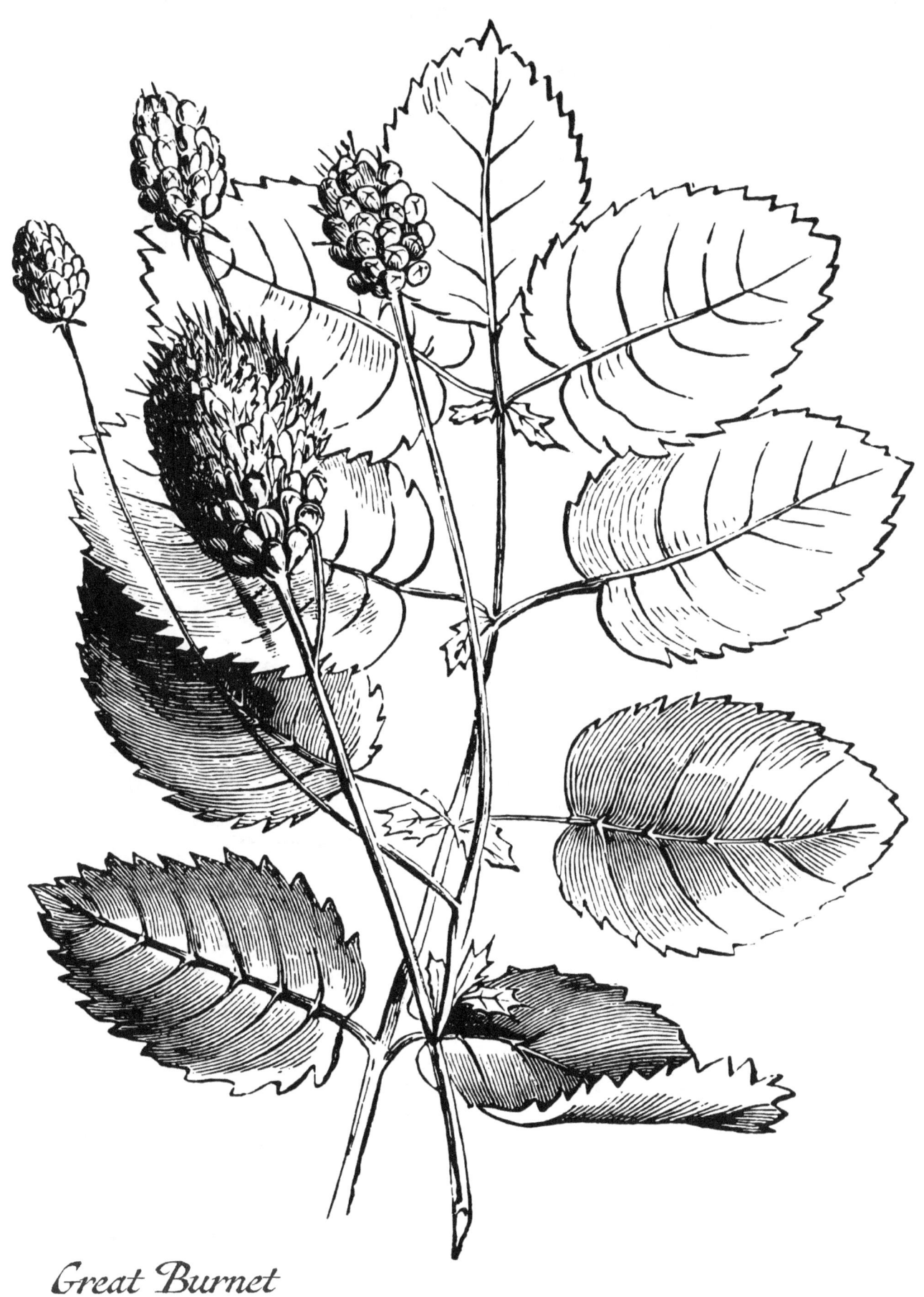

Great Burnet

*Lady's Smock*

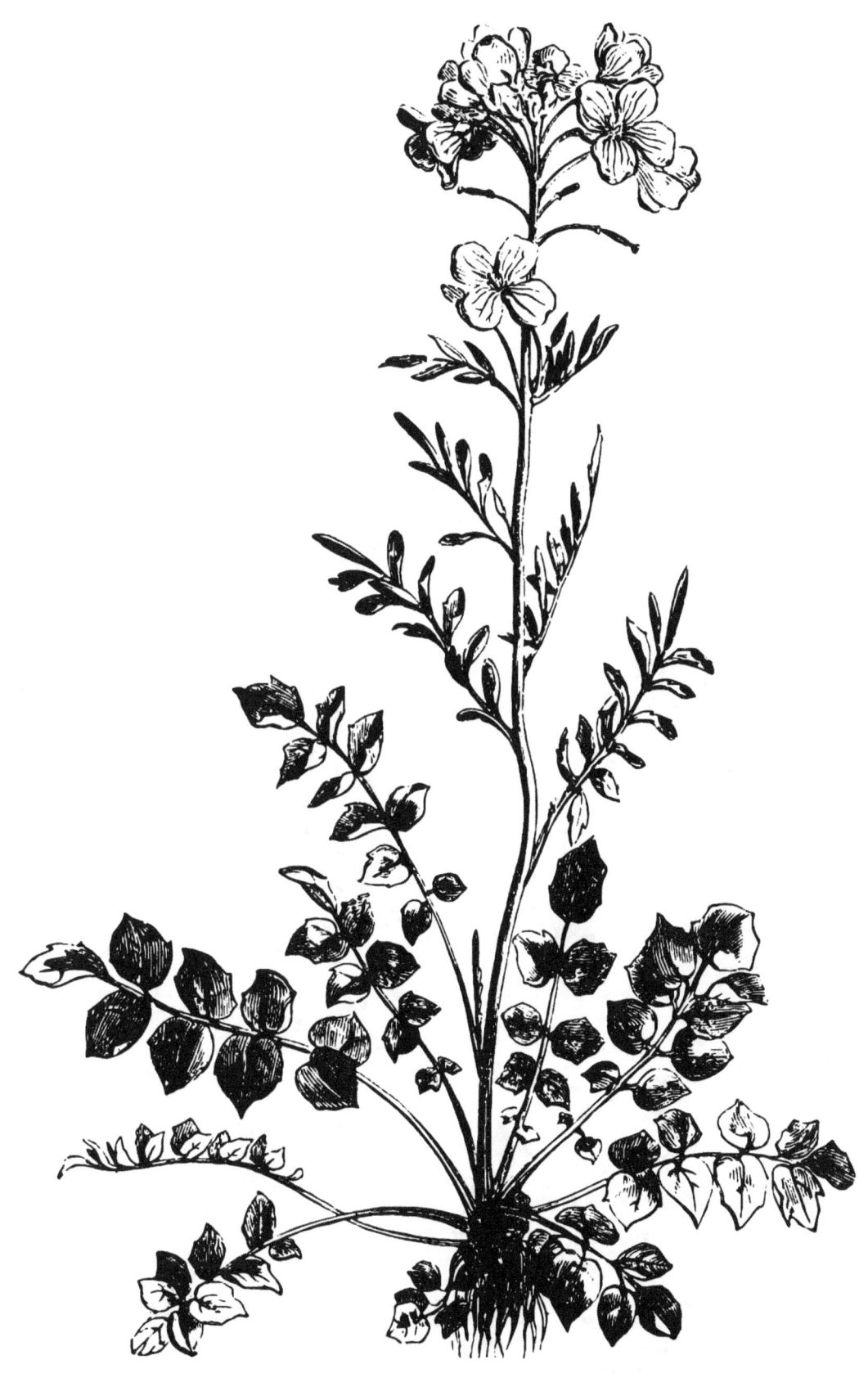

# Hawthorn

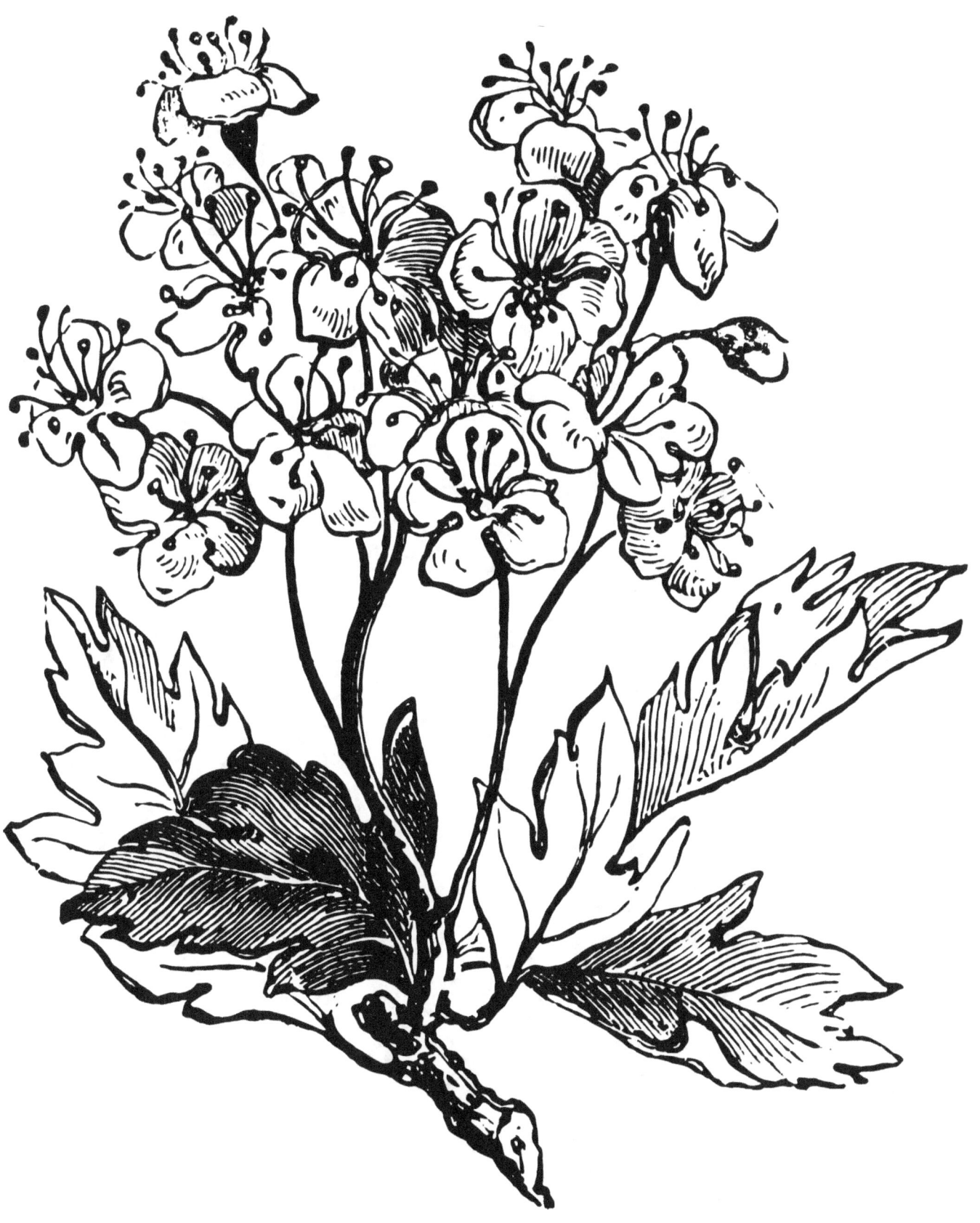

# Blackberry

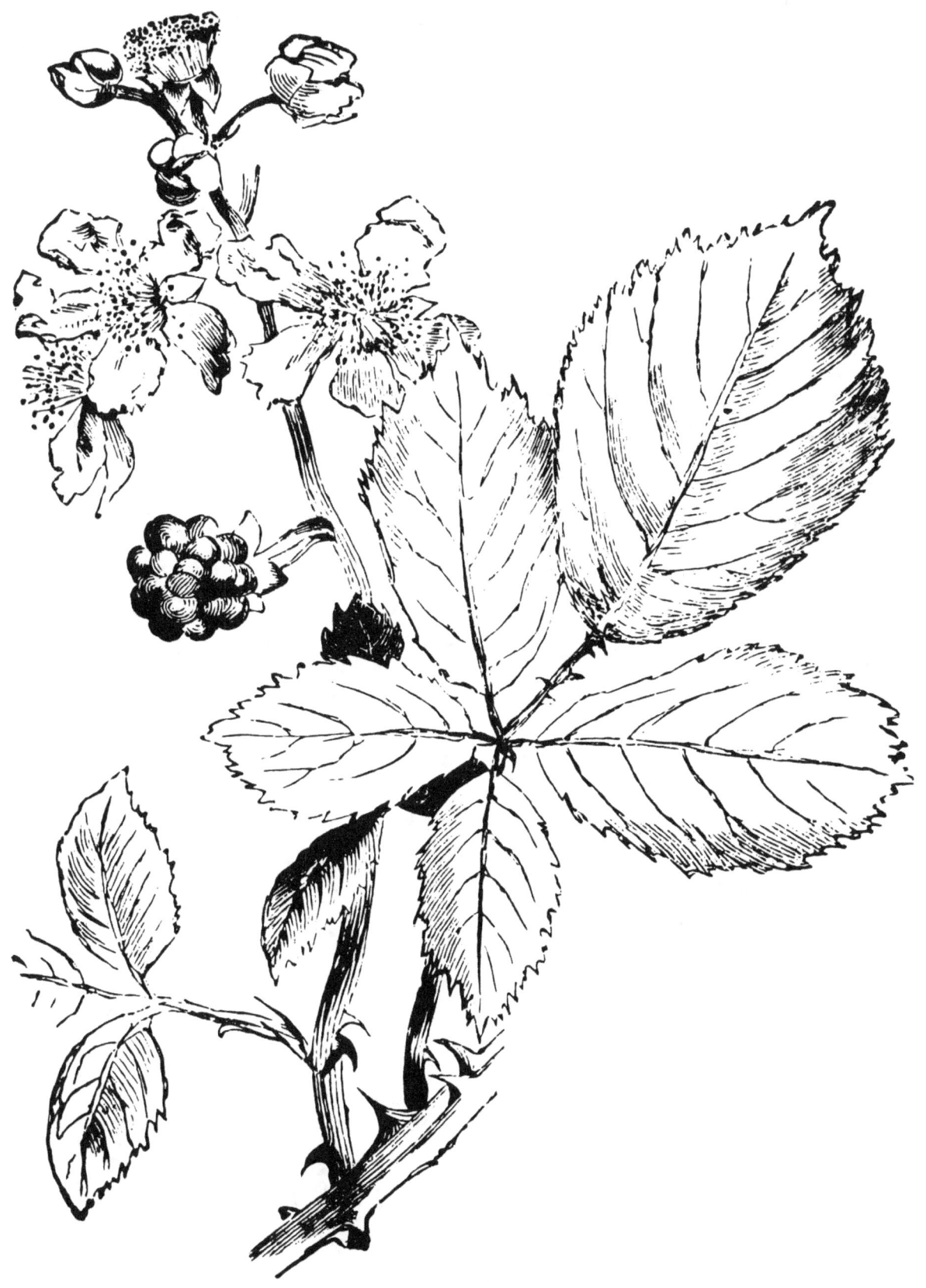

# Common Soapwort

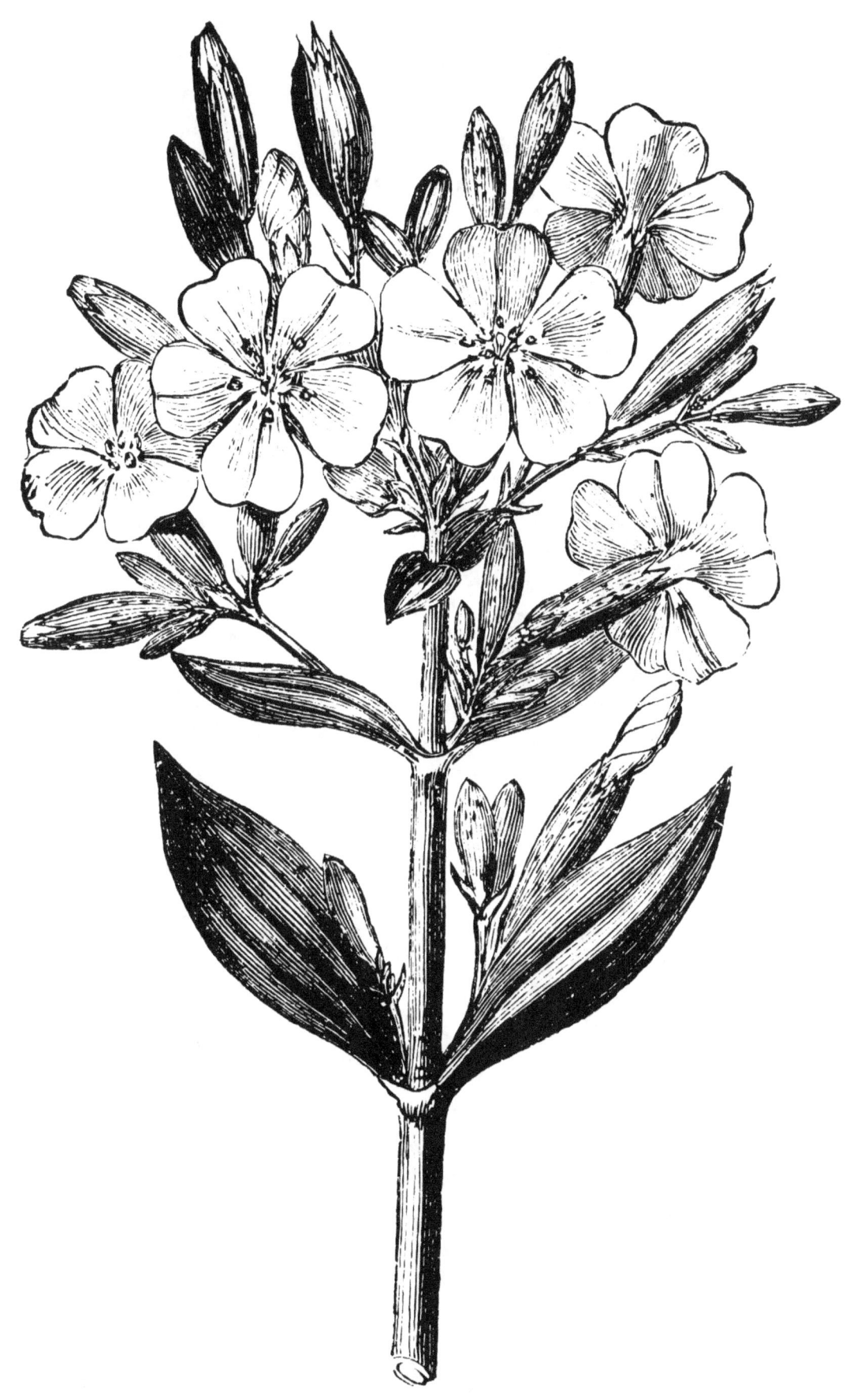

# Common Hemlock

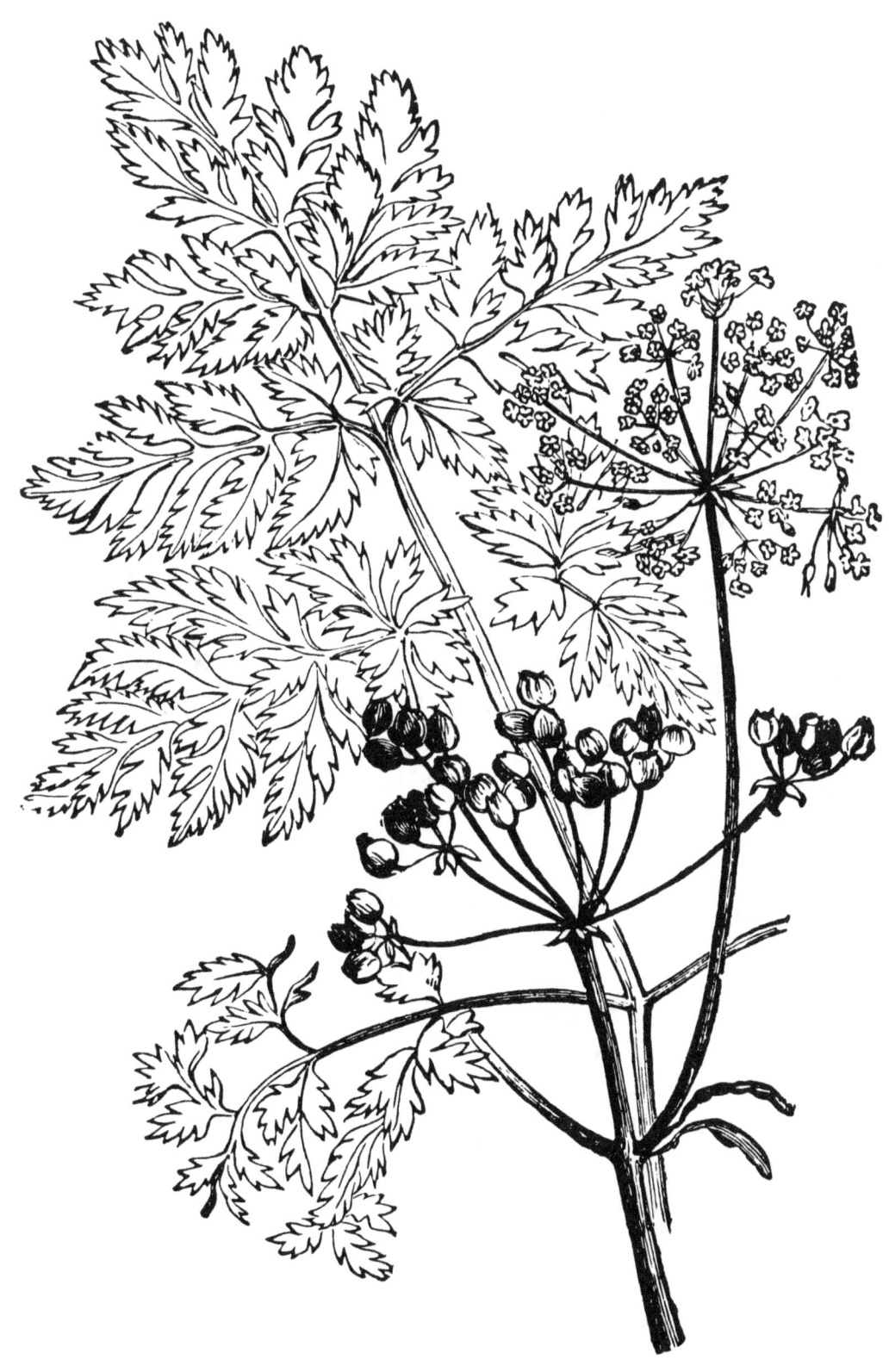

# Common Rock-Rose

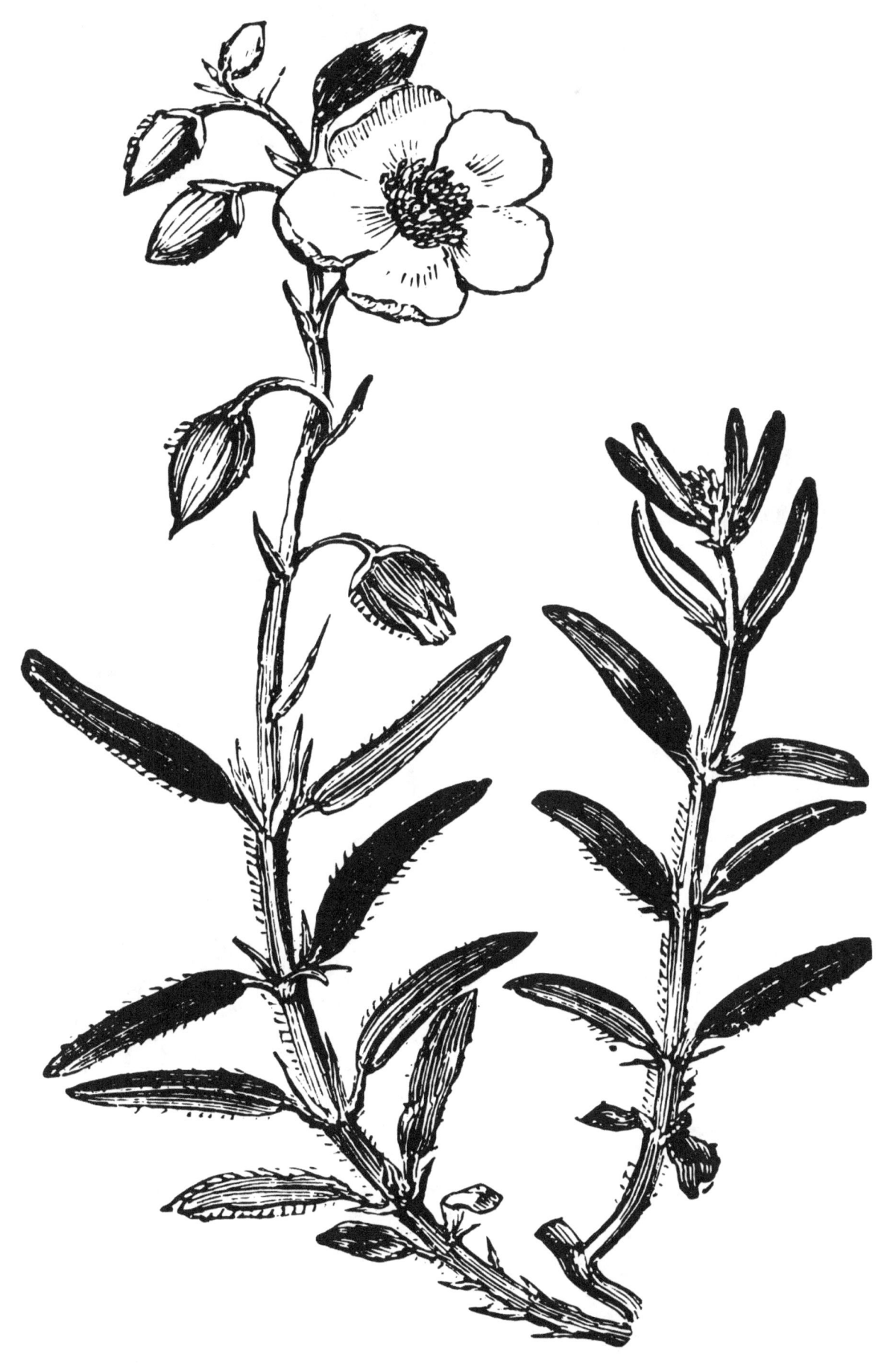

# Cornish Bladder-Seed

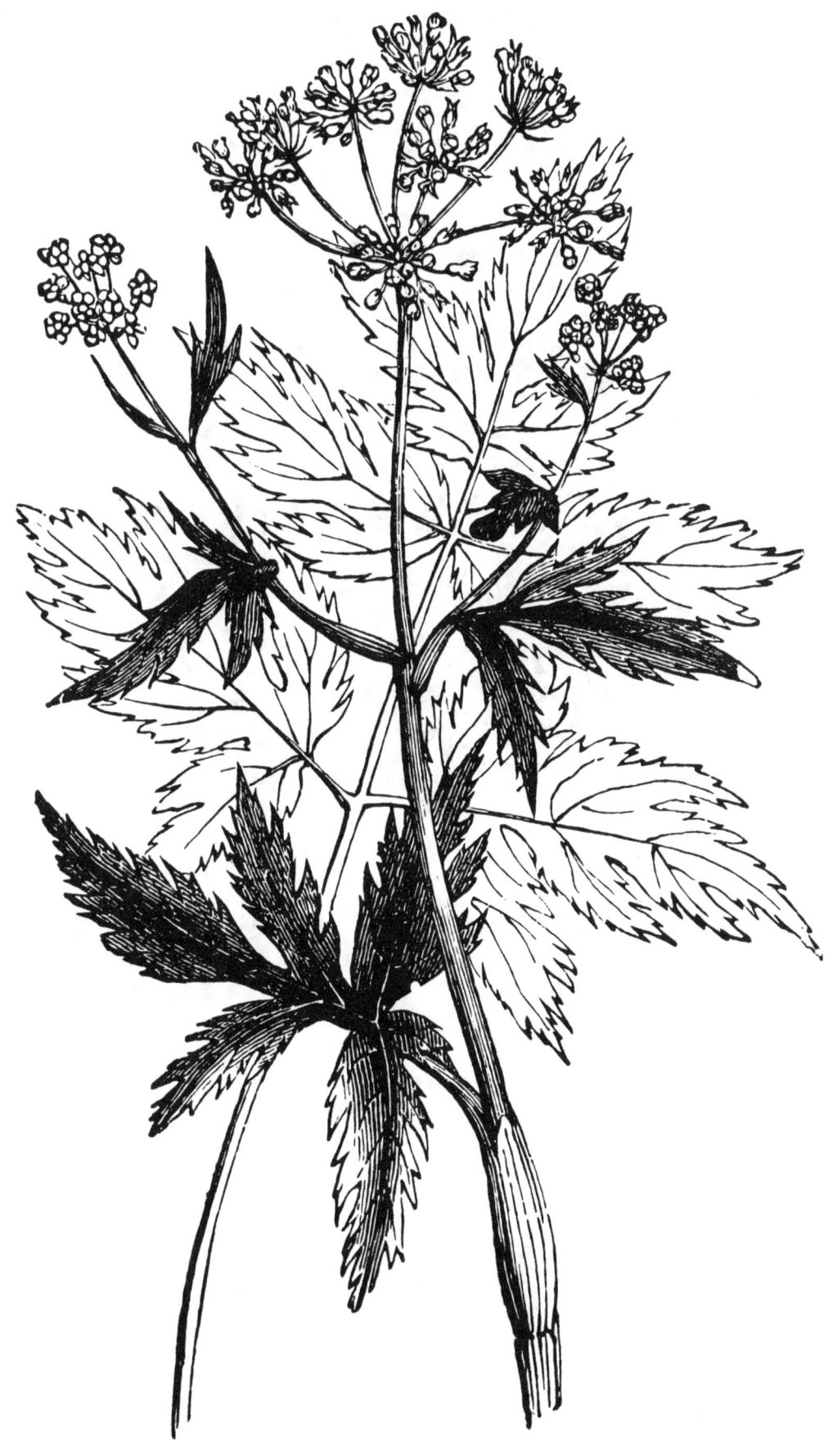

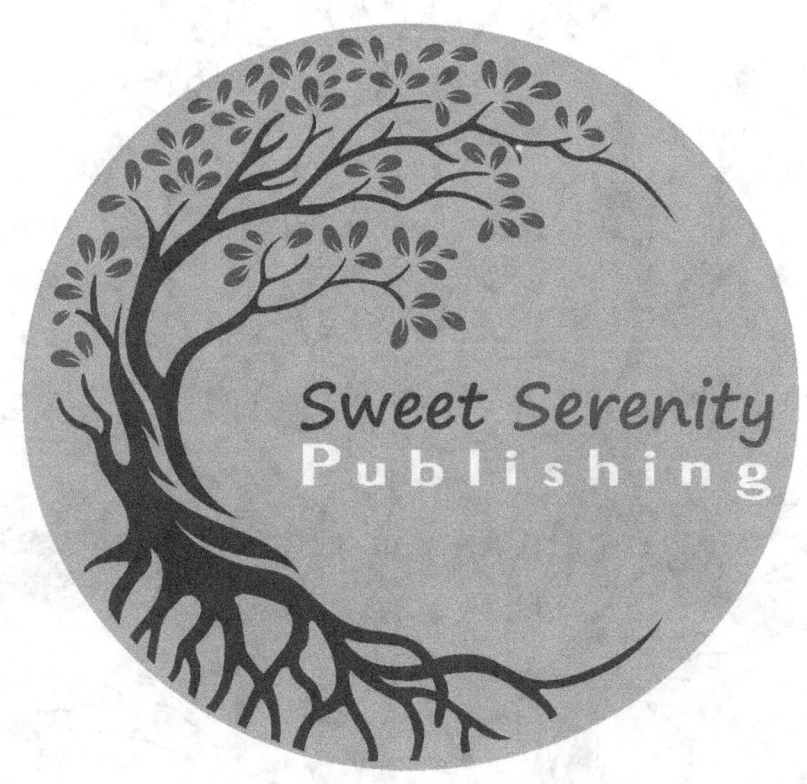

sweetserenitypublishing@gmail.com

www.ingramcontent.com/pod-product-compliance
Lightning Source LLC
Chambersburg PA
CBHW080547220526
45466CB00010B/3069